GW01066411

The
Bioelectrical Investigation
of
SEXUALITY
and
ANXIETY

WILHELM REICH

The
Bioelectrical Investigation
of

SEXUALITY

and

ANXIETY

TRANSLATED FROM THE GERMAN
BY MARION FABER, WITH DEREK AND INGE JORDAN

Edited by Mary Higgins and Chester M. Raphael, M.D.

FARRAR, STRAUS AND GIROUX
NEW YORK

Published simultaneously in Canada by
McGraw-Hill Ryerson Ltd., Toronto

Printed in the United States of America

First printing, 1982

Designed by Irving Perkins

Library of Congress Cataloging in Publication Data
Reich, Wilhelm.
The bioelectrical investigation of sexuality and anxiety.
Contents: The orgasm as an electrophysiological discharge—
Sexuality and anxiety—
The bioelectrical function of sexuality and anxiety.
1. Sex (Psychology)   2. Anxiety.   3. Electrophysiology.
I. Higgins, Mary.
II. Raphael, Chester M.
III. Title.
155.3   81-3209
AACR2

Love, work and knowledge are the wellsprings of our life. They should also govern it.

WILHELM REICH

Contents

Foreword

My experimental studies during the years 1934 to 1938 gradually and logically centered on a single basic problem: how deeply is the function of the orgasm rooted in biology?

This book is composed of three studies from that period. They follow one another in a logical sequence which reflects the various stages of progress made in the development of orgone biophysics, a process which began in 1934 when I achieved a breakthrough into the biological foundation of psychoneuroses.* The present volume can with good reason be understood as a logical continuation of my *Character Analysis*. It is the character analysis of the areas of biological functioning, so to speak. The discovery of biological energy, the orgone, was made solely as a result of the consistent and logical nature of the sex-economic theory of the biopsychic apparatus. At certain places in these studies, which were completed before 1939—i.e., before the discovery of the orgone—the reader will find statements and assumptions which were later fully confirmed by the previously unknown orgonotic pulsation function. The relevant places are marked by footnotes [1945].

The logic of the development of sex-economy into orgone biophysics is objective proof of its unbiased nature. If someone traversing unknown territory concludes from seemingly unimportant signs that a huge lake is nearby, and then, following these signs, actually comes to a great lake, that

* Cf. "Psychic Contact and Vegetative Current" [Chapter XIII in *Character Analysis*].

is proof enough that he has observed and interpreted the signs correctly.

Orgone biophysics is firmly based on the foundation of direct observation, experimental testing of these observations, logical development of experiments, and interpretations that keep pace with the work process. It fills many gaps in natural science; for the first time, objective natural processes are concretely linked with subjective emotional life.

W. R.

1945

The
Bioelectrical Investigation
of
SEXUALITY
and
ANXIETY

1

The Orgasm as an Electrophysiological Discharge*

Although in his compilation *Die Lebensnerven* (3rd ed., Springer, 1930) Müller makes general mention of the relationship between orgasm and the contraction of the smooth muscles, the physiology of orgastic excitation has remained unexplained. To my knowledge, there have been no experiments on animals or humans. Various disorders are described in the sexological literature, but they are not considered in the context of how they relate to unconscious psychic life, or to the physiology of the sexual function, or to the social conditions of people's sex lives.

An orgasm is more complete and provides greater release the more the sexual excitation has been concentrated in the genitals and the more completely this excitation then ebbs away within the vegetative nervous system. The nature of this excitation is crucially important to the understanding of sexuality in general.

In the clinical treatment of neuroses and sexual disorders, orgasm is found to be a process of excitation which is characterized by the complete reduction of all psychic activity to vegetative tension and relaxation. We came to understand "orgastic potency" as the ability to allow, free of all inhibitions, a relaxation of the corresponding tension

* First published in German, in unrevised form, in Reich's *Journal for Political Psychology and Sex-Economy*, Copenhagen, 1934.

that has accumulated in the biophysical apparatus, and to experience it fully.

The following questions must be answered:

Is sexual tension nothing more than a mechanical phenomenon?

Is sexual stasis, then, an essentially mechanical process?

Is the relaxation that occurs with orgasm a mechanical relief, resulting from the emptying of engorged seminal vesicles or sperm ducts, as many opinions would have it, or does it involve merely a mechanical change in the surface tension of the sex organs?

These and similar questions demand an answer, for neuroses cannot be properly treated or prevented in the context of social sex-economy until these problems have been adequately settled. If the theory of sex-economy is correct in contending that orgastic potency is the key to understanding the economy and dynamics of emotional life in general and of psychic disorders in particular, then one must understand the orgasm problem in order to understand neuroses, and vice versa.

SOME PECULIAR FEATURES OF SEXUALITY

The assumption that sexual tension and relaxation are purely mechanical processes leaves unexplained many facts, which fit easily and without contradiction into an overall understanding if one assumes that, besides mechanical relaxation, a *bioelectrical discharge* occurs during orgasm, something which ought to be verifiable by experiment.

To start with, it might seem as if *mechanical relaxation* is restricted to men only and is not a valid explanation in the case of women. It is this mechanical view of events which led to the idea, predominant in sexology, that it is "natural" for women not to experience orgasm. The sociological origin of this idea has been reported in detail elsewhere.*

Orgastic phenomena in the healthy woman, which fully resemble those of the man, thus require explanation. Women are able to experience the same kind of rhythmic-clonic convulsions of the involuntary muscles; they experience peripheral concentration of excitation before climax and centripetal draining and ebbing away of excitation after climax, exactly the way men do.

In *coitus interruptus* a complete mechanical discharge takes place and often excitation at climax is even more intense than usual; nevertheless, there is an abiding sensation of not being satisfied or of having experienced inadequate relaxation, if any at all.

In *coitus condomatus*, too, a mechanical discharge takes place, while gratification is greatly diminished. This cannot be explained by the reduction in tactile sensations, for pure touch sensation is present; but the sensation of pleasure is lacking or reduced, and it is precisely this that needs to be explained. Unambiguous signs of stasis such as irritability, anxiety, lack of interest in work, which tend in time to accompany coitus condomatus, point to the lack of adequate relaxation.

Clinical investigations show that, depending on the type of female secretion, two fundamentally different tactile sensations of excitation occur during the sexual act, whether it is performed with the same partner or with different partners. Patients describe one kind of sensation as "watery" or "squishy," the other as "oily" or "thick and abundant." The first imparts less intense and qualitatively

* C.f. Reich, *Die Sexualität im Kulturkampf*, 2nd ed., Sexpol-Verlag, 1936. [*The Sexual Revolution* (New York: Farrar, Straus and Giroux, 1974) —Ed.]

different sensations, compared to the second. The differences probably arise from, on the one hand, more serous or, on the other, more colloidal secretion in the female genital glands.

Probably the most striking fact is the relationship between genital friction and the contraction of the genital muscles. Their tone is greatly increased during erection. In addition, any friction produces an involuntary contraction, unless one voluntarily tenses against it. With increasing friction, the involuntary muscle contractions increase in intensity. As the climax approaches, the contractions become *clonic;* i.e., several spontaneous muscle contractions follow each other in quick succession, and they cannot voluntarily be inhibited, even when the friction has stopped. While up to the point where clonus occurs, friction causes the muscles to contract, from that moment on, the clonus of the genital muscles seems to determine the contraction of the voluntarily innervated muscle systems of the abdominal wall, legs, face, and arms. This is the central aspect of the "spread of excitation throughout the body."

We must explain why orgastically impotent compulsive characters experience no gratification despite mechanical release; and why friction exerted on the spermatic duct and pelvic floor does not trigger any muscular contractions in patients suffering from the inability to ejaculate.

The fact that sexual compatibility exists between certain men and certain women is a very remarkable phenomenon which until now has remained completely unexplained and has merely been glorified in mystical terms. It is a mutual attraction and, as it later turns out, a compatibility in sexual rhythm, which often operates at first sight without either of the individuals being aware of it. If one disregards genital compatibility (which cannot be the reason for the phenomenon), psychic characteristics, appearance, etc., one arrives at the conclusion that there is something, which laymen tend to label "sexual aura" or "sex appeal." These spontaneous unconscious object choices tend to prove "harmonious" if no serious complications intervene. The actual nature of this harmony, however, remains unexplained.* The fact that people who lack free-flowing sexuality are felt to be "unattractive" by persons with strongly erotic natures is part of the same problem.

When the male member touches the moist mucous membrane of the female vagina, a difficult-to-control urge arises to make complete contact between the penis and the surface of the vagina. The man feels driven to penetrate completely and the woman to accept him fully. (In contrast to this "genital magnet effect," as we might call it, speaking for the moment simply metaphorically, orgastically impotent men and frigid women exhibit no such urge, or only a very diminished one, despite vaginal lubrication; or else such people act with conscious intent, knowing that one "should" penetrate and accept, respectively.) A further indication of this remarkable phenomenon is that withdrawal of the member means overcoming a resistance which is a physically unpleasurable stimulus to the point of being painful. This sensation is particularly pronounced when withdrawal takes place at climax, the height of excitation. Then the pleasurable muscular contraction begins to produce pain. It is the same with patients who voluntarily or unconsciously tense the muscles of the pelvic floor and genitals too much during intercourse and are then overwhelmed by excitation. Such people tend to develop a great fear of the sexual act and the excitation.

If the female genital organ is dry, the sexual act pro-

---

* Since 1939, the existence of "biosexual contact" has been confirmed and explained by the function of the contact of two fields of orgonotic excitation.

duces nothing more than ordinary tactile pleasure, even if friction leads to mechanical relaxation in the man.

Onanistic gratification is reduced when friction is produced with a dry hand rather than one moistened with saliva. A therapist must be aware of this if he wishes to improve the genitality of impotent men. Likewise, when using a condom, the sensation is greater if the condom is moistened inside.

It is not immediately apparent why gentle and slow friction produces an incomparably stronger sensation than vigorous and rapid friction. This cannot be explained in tactile, mechanical terms alone.

Detailed inquiries in sex-counseling centers, which are borne out by clinical experience, show that there are two kinds of frictional movements: one is thrusting, strenuous, and executed with the entire torso; the other is more spontaneous, undulating, and limited to the pelvic region. The first occurs in persons with strong muscular armor, as for example in emotionally blocked individuals, who have to actually overcome their vegetative inhibition, etc. The second occurs only in muscularly relaxed and also psychically free-flowing people. We know that the first form is determined by the attempt to compensate for a lack of *spontaneous* movement. What determines the second has yet to be explained.

Let me in conclusion indicate a gap in our understanding of the complex orgasm phenomenon. Following orgastic release, the genitals can suddenly no longer be stimulated, and the mental image of the sexual act cannot be reproduced or is completely without affect. The view that the release is mechanical, based on the vascular congestion of the genital organs, is inadequate, because the hyperemia disappears only very gradually. This seems to be a *consequence* of the sudden drop in excitation, rather than its cause. If one wished to explain the phenomenon in terms of neuronal sensitivity, one would first have to explain why the end-organs become refractory precisely after discharge.

All the phenomena enumerated here can be understood by assuming that the orgasm represents a *bioelectrical* discharge. To my knowledge, this view is new in scientific research, although here and there it is accepted as a fact in popular belief. If it is correct, we must first of all demonstrate and clarify the relationship of mechanical relaxation to bioelectrical discharge.

THE ORGASM FORMULA:

Mechanical tension → bioelectrical charge → bioelectrical discharge → mechanical relaxation

The orgastic function must be part of the natural order of things, and in fact an elemental part. The basic function of all living matter, namely tension and relaxation, charge and discharge, is represented here in its purest form. It also combines two fundamental directions of vegetative flow which we will discuss in detail later. Orgastic discharge produces a feeling of pleasure and fusion with the object; its blocking, on the other hand, produces a feeling of anxiety and separation from the object. The orgastic function also represents one of the most important nodal points of the body-soul problem.

Vegetative excitation of the genitals is the first requirement of the orgastic function. The erection is essentially an intense filling of the genital blood vessels, beginning with the genital arteries (parasympathetic effect). The genital muscles, too (M. ischocavernosus and bulbocavernosus), are parasympathetically excited, resulting in increased tonus. This causes a compression of the efferent blood vessels (venous plexus), located closer to the surface than the arteries. (The antithesis is sympathetic, anxious excitation which contracts the arteries and renders the genital muscles flaccid, thus impeding the erection.) The more completely this excitation takes over, the more constricted the urethra becomes; that is to say, the stronger the tone of the peripheral genital muscles, the stronger must be the subsequent contractions of those muscles, which propel the semen through the barrier of muscles and vessels.

In women, the erection process is in principle the same as in men. Here, too, arterial hyperemia and secondary venous congestion of the corpora cavernosa clitoridis and of the bulbo vestibuli (the vascular spaces around the clitoris and around the orifice of the vagina) occur.

Thus, we must distinguish between the following elements of mechanical tension: in men, the tension in the seminal vesicles and the spermatic ducts; in both sexes, the tension due to heightened "turgor" of the genital glands and tissues; the tension arising from engorgement of the corpora cavernosa; the tension of the skin and mucous membranes.

The well-known sensation of tension in the genitals during sexual excitation thus has a direct mechanical basis; i.e., the heightened mechanical tension of the tissues. The symptomatology of sexual disorders, especially female disorders, has shown that any voluntary tensing of the striated genital muscles either impedes gratification or makes it completely impossible. This means that overcoming the mechanical tension through the process now to be described is all the more pleasurable, and the excitation is quantitatively more intense, the more relaxed the person's state.

The next question is, how does relaxation come about after parasympathetic excitation has produced mechanical tension. Let us remind ourselves of the evidence, described earlier as problematic, that friction results in *involuntary* contractions of the smooth and striated genital musculature. Any friction—i.e., any change in the surface contact between the vaginal mucosa and the penis—produces a muscle contraction in healthy individuals. During resting contact—i.e., when there is no motion—no contraction occurs (except at the end stage), and in fact the tonus may decrease.

We know that a muscle reacts with a twitch to galvanic stimuli both when the electric current is applied and when it is removed ("closing" and "opening" twitch). The striated muscle contracts quickly and relaxes just as quickly; the smooth muscle, on the other hand, contracts in a long-drawn-out wave. We are thus forced to conclude that muscle contractions due to friction are the same as those that occur in electrically stimulated muscles. As the frequency and intensity of friction increase, the waves of contraction increase; and when the transition is made to the climax, tetany—i.e., a prolonged spasm at the height of contraction—occurs, just as it does when a quick succession of electrical stimuli is applied. This tetany is then released, with or without further friction, in a muscle clonus; i.e., a series of involuntary automatic contractions of all the genital muscles. It is not the tetanic contraction but this clonus which constitutes orgasm and brings about release of tension; the contractions recede and give way to a feeling of complete relaxation followed by sleepiness. It is now clear what brings about the ejaculation of semen and release of tension: during orgasm, all the excitation or tension which has been built up as a result of the preceding stimulation (friction) is discharged in several spontaneous muscle contractions, which are no longer dependent on stimulation; energy is dissipated and a state of rest follows.

With the powerful clonic muscle contraction, the semen

in the male is transported out of the reservoirs, through the barrier of the tonically contracted penile musculature, and thus provides a secondary, mechanical discharge. In the same way that mechanical tension was needed for the electrical charge to build up in the genital organs, so electrical discharge is now the determining condition for mechanical relaxation. Since this reciprocal relationship between mechanical and electrical processes represents the actual orgastic process, we will call it the *"tension-charge process"* or the *"discharge-relaxation process,"* which together constitute the orgasm.

The essence of the gratifying relaxation is not the mechanical but rather the bioelectrical discharge, as it is manifested in the muscle contractions. Even slight electric voltages are enough to produce a discharge of semen in the male. Gratification, however, is not dependent on ejaculation; rather, its intensity is proportional to the preceding mechanical tension, to the resulting electrical charge, and to the resistance which must be overcome when the transition is made to the clonic state. For that reason, ejaculation during sleep or with partial erection produces little or no pleasure or relaxation. Relaxation is, therefore, all the more complete the greater the preceding tension of the erection has been. And thus, one of the most significant characteristics of orgastic potency is the rhythm and force of ejaculation, not the ejaculation per se.

Measuring the amount of charge and discharge in healthy people during intercourse would be a very important aid to understanding the pathology of a number of disorders of the vegetative functions. Unfortunately, there are—at the present time, at least—great obstacles barring this approach. Aesthetic considerations would not have to come into it; often, what is considered aesthetic today may be regarded as narrow-minded tomorrow. It is not aesthetic problems but those of a technical nature which stand in the way of such a study: the subjects' awareness of the measuring procedure would falsify the results. *C'est tout!* Yet, on the basis of the measurements that have been possible up to now, we can safely say the following:

In the sexual act, two bioelectrically highly charged organisms come into contact with one another.* The higher psychic functions cease temporarily. Everything is concentrated on the discharge of vegetative high tension. Two bodies experiencing orgastic ecstasy are nothing more than a quivering mass of plasm. Anyone who considers this assertion an "insult to his sense of delicacy" simply reveals his own unnaturalness. Whatever force is capable of forging people and all living nature into *one* is infinitely broader in scope and on a higher plane than decadent drawing-room philosophizing about the unattainable. We are concerned here with very practical questions about life.

The arrangement of membranes, boundary surfaces, and fluids during sexual intercourse indicates that a complete electrolytic system has been established. The surface of the penis must be seen as one electrode and the vaginal mucosa as the other. The contact between the two is made by the acidic female secretion acting as an electrolyte. Water, which does not conduct, is not an electrolyte. Saliva, on the other hand, does conduct. It is no coincidence that, as clinical experience has shown, sexual sensation declines

---

* [1945] This view preceded the later *orgone-physical* discovery that intercourse involves excitation and contact, the *radiation* of body cells, and the *fusion* of two "orgonotic systems." In the interest of illustrating the *development* of orgone biophysics, the following, no longer valid, electrophysiological explanation of the sexual act, as arrived at in 1935, will be given.

when the vaginal mucous membrane is moistened with
water; saliva, on the other hand, enhances sensation, although not to the same degree as vaginal secretion, which
is a colloidal-acidic solution. As we know, the intensity of
pleasurable sensation depends on the ratio of the colloidal
to the aqueous portion of the secretion:

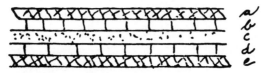

a—male circulation
b—male boundary surface (skin of penis)
c—female secretion (conductor-electrolyte)
d—female boundary surface (vaginal mucosa)
e—female circulation

If one regards the sexual act as essentially an electrical
process, the phenomenon of the genital "magnet effect" as
well as the muscle contractions due to friction becomes
understandable. In accordance with the laws of physics,
the difference in potential between two charged surfaces
in contact with each other will equal itself out to a greater
or lesser extent depending on the size of the contact area
(the larger the area, the greater the degree of equalization). In consequence, the urge toward complete contact
of the genital surfaces—i.e., toward complete penetration
or complete acceptance of the male member—is explained
by the partial relaxation which facilitates complete contact,
and by the tension of the parts not in contact. Thus, we have
to distinguish between two kinds of pleasure: first, that
arising from partial relaxation during resting contact which

is a model of end-pleasure, when the entire charge is dissipated and relaxation is complete; second, the pleasure arising from friction, i.e., pleasure which is caused by stimulation and the muscular contraction connected with it. This motor pleasure, too, which is surely a model of any kind of muscular-motor pleasure, anticipates a process that occurs completely during orgastic clonus. The first type of pleasure can be called "relaxation pleasure," and the second "tension pleasure." The first is an important result of lowering potential and the second of raising it. The process is clearly manifest in the case of resting contact during coitus, when tensions are being equalized, and after the orgasm, when release of tension is complete.

The nature of tension pleasure is less clear. According to our assumptions, tension should produce unpleasure and not pleasure, which we generally think of as an expression of the release of tension. If tension has been built up by friction, it largely dissipates when the genitalia remain in full contact for a while without friction. It then rises again when friction recommences. This tension is experienced as pleasurable. How can we reconcile the increase in tension with its accompanying pleasure ("tension pleasure")? No doubt the potential surfaces are recharged with each friction; but just as surely, the accompanying contraction of the muscles dissipates the accumulated energy, and this contracting makes the increased tension pleasurable instead of unpleasurable. We can mention two facts which support this assertion. First, without touching on our problem, F. Kraus concludes from his studies that the nerve acquires tension during excitation, while the contracting muscle discharges the stored excitation. When friction occurs, the interface and the various parts of the vegetative system build up energy, while the contracting genital muscles discharge energy. Forepleasure, then, would seem to consist of a simultaneous charge and partial discharge. I put forward this hypothesis in 1923 in my work "Zur Trieb-energetik,"* simply on the basis of the phenomenology of the sexual act. Forepleasure can thus be understood as a functional process which offers an explanation for the pleasurable nature of tension. Second, it is striking that eroto-genic (perverse) masochists experience each intensification of pleasure brought about through friction as unpleasurable, which thus forces them to avoid it. One is also struck by the fact that a basic characteristic of perverse masochists is that they voluntarily tense their genital muscles and thereby prevent involuntary friction-induced contractions. This proves that without the frictional contraction the fric-tion by itself as a pure charging process is unpleasurable and is therefore avoided (as, for example, incessant tick-ling).

End-pleasure, in contrast to forepleasure, is pure pleasure. It is based solely on muscular discharge, which also reduces nervous excitation in a manner which is still completely unexplained. This last assumption has to be made, for after orgasm the nervous system is incapable of becoming re-charged. For a while no mental image and no friction is capable of recharging the vegetative system. The surfaces of the genitals also fail to respond to stimulation. The pos-sibility of a new charge must, however, be linked with the relaxation. The fact that regular, gratifying sexual inter-course develops greater orgastic potency is evidence of this, as is also the fact that infrequent gratification causes potency disorders.

---

* "Concerning the Energy of Drives." [Included in *Early Writings, Volume One* (New York: Farrar, Straus and Giroux, 1975)—Ed.]

Frigid women lack not only involuntary muscular contractions, because they voluntarily tense all their muscles, but also frictional tension is missing, because of dryness of the vagina mucosa.

In patients suffering from premature ejaculation, the genital muscles involuntarily begin to twitch too soon (intermittent ejaculation) or to contract tonically (flow of semen only). In these cases, excitation is probably transmitted too soon from the vegetative nervous system to the muscles; but the physiology of the process is very unclear.

There are fundamental differences also in the sexual behavior of both sexes which are based on the differences in their orgastic potency. It appears that people who are able to experience frictionally induced orgastic twitching movements are much more capable of maintaining monogamous relationships than people who experience only the sensations stemming from mechanical release. The monogamous behavior is based neither on the inhibition of polygamous impulses nor on moral considerations, but on the sex-economic principle of genuine pleasure which is repeatedly experienced. The basis for such pleasure is full sexual harmony with the partner. There is no difference between men and women in this respect. If, on the other hand, a suitable partner is lacking, which is usually the case given the prevailing conditions of sexual life, then the capacity for monogamy turns into its opposite; namely, an unremitting search for a suitable sex object. This kind of polygamous behavior is in no way to be considered neurotic; but if the stasis persists, it can lead to neurosis. This behavior is not based on sexual repression but, on the contrary, on natural sexual impulses. If the right partner is found, monogamous behavior reasserts itself automatically and continues for as long as the sexual compatibility and gratification last. Thoughts and desires centered on other partners are either very weak or else, again for sex-economic reasons, they are not acted upon. This is the case as long as another partner is not thought sexually equal or superior to the first, a fact which is clearly sensed. However, the old relationship breaks down totally when a new one promises greater pleasure. This fact is hopelessly at odds with the entire sexual organization of modern society, where material conditions and consideration for children run counter to the sex-economic principle. Under the conditions of the sex-denying social order, it is precisely the healthiest people who are subjected in this way to the greatest suffering.

People who are orgastically disturbed, and thus incapable of electric charge and discharge, behave differently. Since they experience less pleasure during intercourse, they are either in a better position to do without a sexual partner for short or long periods, or else they are less discriminating; sex does not mean very much to them. If they are polygamous, it is due to a defective sexual structure. They always exhibit more or less deeply rooted disorders in their work performance, which is not the case with the former type. They are better able to adapt to the conditions of marriage. However, their fidelity is not based on sexual gratification but on moral inhibitions; i.e., not on sex-economic principles but on principles of compulsory sexual morality. They are always subject to neurotic regression to childhood conflicts. Their polygamy is not very gratifying, and if the condition continues for a long time, they become increasingly unable to find a suitable sex partner. They are often better able to comply with the demands of bourgeois society, but at the same time they pay for this compliance by developing neurotic disorders which affect all members of the family, especially the children. This is erroneously viewed as the effect of "heredity." If they undergo vegetotherapy,* and it is successful in establishing orgastic potency, their behavior is transformed and they begin to develop all the attributes of the genital character.

Orgasm is an elementary natural phenomenon; it governs all living creatures who have the capacity for vegetative expansion and contraction. The tension → charge → discharge → relaxation process which has been revealed and which governs the orgasm requires extremely precise study. First, we must discover in which fundamental vegetative phenomena of life it is rooted. Then we must prove it experimentally.

Let us now turn to the relationships between sexual excitation and anxiety.

---

* Reich applied this term to the therapeutic technique he developed after his discovery of muscular armor and the orgasm reflex (1935). It indicated his shift of emphasis from the psychological to the physiological and the fact that this technique directly influenced the functioning of the vegetative nervous system.—Ed.

2

*Sexuality and Anxiety**

THE BASIC ANTITHESIS OF
VEGETATIVE LIFE

STARTING POINT AND FUNDAMENTAL IDEAS

Sexual excitation and anxiety are to be regarded as antithetical functions of living matter in general, as well as of
the psychic apparatus in particular. They form a *basic antithesis,* from which the higher functions of the drive apparatus are secondarily derived. Every motor impulse which
serves to bring the bioapparatus closer to the outside world
is functionally identical with sexual excitation. *The available facts permit us to see in sexual excitation the basic
function of life energy per se.* Anxiety, as a primary, irre-
ducible reaction of living matter, is the fundamental antithesis to sexual excitation. Thus, there is a *functional
dualism* in living matter in general and in the psychic apparatus in particular.

Clinical sex-economic experience has proved that "functional" and "somatic" processes are identical. This is at vari-
ance with the three old and fundamental ideas about the
relationship between psychic and physical life which can
be formulated as follows:

* First published in German, in unrevised form, in Reich's *Journal for Political Psychology and Sex-Economy,* Copenhagen, 1934.

21

1. The soul builds the body for itself. It is eternal, absolute, "primary" (metaphysical idealism).
2. The soul is a secretion of the brain (mechanical vulgar materialism).
3. The psychic and physical phenomena make up two independent causal series which are "interrelated" (psychophysical parallelism).

We will combine the dynamics of psychic and physical phenomena into a functional psychophysical identity. It seems just as senseless to speak of two separate, autonomous, self-regulated processes as it is to speak of a one-sided dependence of the one on the other. Instead, we must prove that the basic physical and psychic functions which we can elucidate are totally *identical*. However, under certain circumstances, they also contrast with each other as opposite-acting functions; thus, they may become a *functional antagonistic duality*.

Biofunction

(Psychic and physical functions are identical)

One is justified in inquiring what use a new speculation about the body-soul relationship, this time a *functional* one, is supposed to have for our understanding of nature. There is, after all, no dearth of such studies. I would not hesitate to agree with this view, and would indeed not have undertaken a purely speculative study. In the course of investigating the basic functions of sexuality, however, I found time and again that confusion about the relationship between the psychic and physical functions of sexuality gives rise to typical misconceptions. In addition, some fundamental clinical observations made it possible, as will be seen below, to pave the way to understanding the psychophysical boundary zone. The function of the orgasm cannot be understood in any other way.

It would not be amiss to say a few words about the method by which we dare to approach this most delicate of all areas; namely, the boundary between the psychic and the physical. Our starting point is the dynamic structure of the individual, as revealed through character analysis.

Certain areas of scientific sex-economic research are easily delimited. Research on the interrelationships between individual psychic functions is the proper domain of clinical structural psychology. If one traces the social origin of the questions which result from the moral code, one arrives at sociology; namely, the study of the laws which govern social existence. If, on the other hand, one traces unconscious psychic life down to the depths from which drives originate, one arrives at the physiological and biological. Here the psychological boundaries become blurred, and we encounter, ever more clearly and inescapably, phenomena which, while they play a central role in psychology and even constitute its scientific core, cannot in the final analysis be grasped in psychological terms. One such phenomenon is the *quantity of excitations*, whose interplay is the basic

question of psychic dynamics. Other examples are the problem of the affects attached to ideas and perceptions, the
changeover of the sexual affect into anxiety affect or hate
affect, etc. To understand the psychophysical boundary
area, we must first understand the nature of the drives and
affects themselves. While biology and physiology try to
advance, so to speak, from the physical person to the more
complicated "higher" psychic functions, structural psychology proceeds in the opposite direction, by reducing
complicated psychic phenomena to their simplest laws and
returning to their origins, the drives. Sex-economy pursues
the study of these "drives" into the realm of physiology,
since as a science of the laws of sexuality it must transcend
the borders of the psychic realm. If they proceed correctly,
physiological and psychological research are bound to come
together in certain areas. One such area is the *vegetative
nervous system*, with its links to the basic biological functions on the one hand and psychic mechanisms on the other.

We still have to say a few words about the method by
which sex-economy assumes the right to move on from the
psychology of sexuality to invade the physiological area.
Functional observation teaches us that the psychic apparatus grows out of the biophysiological apparatus and
obeys therefore two different kinds of laws. First, there
are the laws that it has in common with its biophysiological
substrate; e.g., the law of tension and relaxation, of re-
sponding to stimuli, etc. Second, there are the laws that
differentiate it from and contrast it with the physiological
realm, laws which are unique to it and which determine
its characteristic of being opposite to the physical realm.
The repression of drives,* introjection, projection, identifi-

---

* [1945] In the meantime, "muscular armor" has come to be understood
as the biophysical mechanism and background of "emotional repression,"
and has become the basis of the new medical technique of *vegetotherapy.*

cation, etc., belong in this category. If one does not distinguish clearly, along these lines, between psychophysical identity and antithesis, and if one applies the second kind of laws to the physiological realm, one necessarily arrives at false psychologistic results. Since, however, the psychic apparatus is also part of the biophysical apparatus, certain laws which one finds in it must be the same as those that govern the biophysical apparatus. That is especially true for the law of tension and relaxation. Only with the help of such laws common to both areas, but found first in the psychic realm, can one properly advance into the physiological problem areas.

The following investigations are intended to show to what degree this is useful.

SEXUAL EXCITATION AND ANXIETY AFFECT

The problem of anxiety

I will continue the investigation of anxiety at exactly the point where psychoanalytic research left off and got involved in a psychologistic interpretation of physiological processes. At this point the ways of psychoanalysis and of sex-economy diverge irreconcilably.

If one is threatened by a real external danger—e.g., if one is involved in a traffic accident or is attacked by a dog—one experiences an "anxiety state." The same is true when certain patients, such as anxiety hysterics and phobics, suffer a compulsive fantasy—e.g., that a person dear to them might come to harm—although there is no basis for this fear in reality. The first anxiety, which is based on a real situation, is called "real anxiety." The second is referred to as irrational "neurotic anxiety." Analysis of the latter type of anxiety reveals that it is the reaction of the ego to an unconsciously perceived, persistent, and at the same time prohibited drive (e.g., when a mother feels homicidal impulses toward her beloved child). Thus, we speak of drive-induced danger, meaning that even in the case of internal danger there is a reality; namely, that of a drive which is experienced as dangerous and against which the ego defends itself. The difference between real anxiety and neurotic anxiety, then, is that in the former the danger is in the outside world, while in the latter it is within the person himself. What these two types of anxiety have in common is that they are both responses to *real* dangers; for giving in to a prohibited drive would also produce a danger in some form or another and would thus threaten the integrity of the ego. *In the final analysis, neurotic anxiety is also real anxiety.*

But there are also individuals, the stasis neurotics, who suffer from anxiety states but do not link the anxiety with any image, whether conscious or unconscious. *Stasis anxiety is the pure expression of an unrelieved excitation tension.* The fact that neither the inner perception of the excitation nor its motor discharge is permitted results in the excitation tension being converted into anxiety. The difference between stasis anxiety and neurotic anxiety is that no real danger exists. However, in both instances, excitation tension exists. We can also say that stasis anxiety is without content, while neurotic anxiety is linked to certain images.

A further difficulty of the anxiety problem is that in the one case we find anxiety appearing as a consequence of a drive inhibition (stasis anxiety), and in the other case it is the cause of a drive inhibition. Thus, for example, the small boy's anxiety that he will lose his penis is the reason why he represses the impulse to masturbate. On the other hand, the boy develops anxiety after he has suppressed his urge to masturbate, and perhaps develops a fear of the dark. How can anxiety as a cause and anxiety as an effect of a repressed drive be reduced to *one common denominator?* Freud, in *Inhibitions, Symptoms and Anxiety* (1926), reversed his original view that anxiety is a consequence of drive inhibition and stated that it is in fact the actual cause of drive inhibition.* We, on the other hand, are of the opinion that this is not an either-or situation but a process which unites both at one and the same time. To understand this, we have to get away from the imprecise terminology to which we succumb when we speak of "anxiety" in different cases. The boy's anxiety about masturbation, which is due to his belief that something bad could happen to his penis as a result, is not the same as the anxiety affect which he develops *after* he has suppressed the drive impulse. The first may be only a simple fear or merely the apprehension of a danger, and to prevent it he suppresses his drive. We can say that here the anxiety affect never develops beyond an initial stage. In the second, however, it is manifestly fully developed. In the former, the accent is on *apprehension* and in the latter it is on the *anxiety affect*. *Apprehension, which initiates the repression of drive, can only become an anxiety affect if there is already a need-related tension (i.e., sexual stasis).* This is true for every kind of anxiety (including real anxiety).

For example, in homosexuals we observe a castration anxiety which prevents them from having sexual relations with women. But this anxiety does not become an affective anxiety experience until they have remained abstinent for some time. Conversely, erythrophobes lose their anxiety as soon as they fully permit themselves to masturbate, long before they have overcome the fear of being injured in the genitals.

---

* "Repression does not cause anxiety; rather, anxiety is there first; anxiety causes repression" (Freud: *Inhibitions, Symptoms and Anxiety*).

Neurotic anxiety thus arises from an apprehension combined with blocked sexual energy. Just as the defense against an inner drive impulse brings about stasis, and thus the anxiety affect, so conversely the experience of anxiety causes the fixation of drive repression.

What is the relationship of real anxiety to stasis anxiety? Is it possible to reduce these states, which are so different in origin, to one common denominator? Freud denied this possibility and separated stasis anxiety from the other forms of anxiety.* In a real, acute, danger situation, people react with anxiety. Reproducing the situation in the imagination may also help to produce the anxiety affect, depending on the vividness of the mental image. What is the crucial factor that is carried over? *It must be only the affect.* In his vivid recollection of a real danger, the individual behaves as if it were real again. This affect must correspond to a certain physical innervation which came about during the real experience. *Stasis anxiety corresponds to a certain physical innervation.* Are there similarities here, or is there a fundamental difference?

The most important difference is, first, that in the case of stasis anxiety any motility impulse acting from the inside toward the outside is blocked. To use an analogy, it is as if a compressed gas were kept under pressure and it then exerted a counterpressure, which we could equate with stasis. But in the case of real anxiety, most clearly in fright, there is a *rapid withdrawal of all energy into the inside.* The end result is the same, however; namely, an *internal stasis of biological energy.* To remain with the anal-

* "Anxiety as a signal of the ego may [also] be valid in the development of anxiety in the case of anxiety neurosis brought on by somatic damage. But we can no longer maintain that it is the libido itself which is then transformed into anxiety" (Freud: *Inhibitions, Symptoms and Anxiety*).

ogy, it is as if a gas were first in an uncompressed state and an external force then suddenly compressed it. In both cases, we would end up with the same increased pressure, though in the one instance this would have been caused by preventing expansion of the gas and in the other by compressing it. *Real anxiety* and *stasis anxiety* can therefore be reduced to a common denominator; i.e., *blocked excitation*. Normally, real anxiety disperses and does not become fixated. However, it can endure in the form of neurotic anxiety. This happens when actual danger and the excitation stasis resulting from it are absorbed by a preexisting need stasis. This is seen most clearly in traumatic neurosis.

Although we have found the common denominator of all kinds of affective anxiety experiences (fright, real anxiety, neurotic anxiety, stasis anxiety) in excitation stasis, many questions still remain to be answered. What is the relationship of the excitation in neurotic anxiety to that of real anxiety, and how do both relate to the excitation of pure stasis anxiety? Simple analysis shows us the way to this psychophysical boundary zone. *Excitation stasis constitutes a physiological* problem which we can approach from two sides: its subjective inner psychic manifestations and its objective somatic manifestations.

Sexuality and anxiety as opposite excitations of the vegetative life apparatus

By carefully following the manifestations of anxiety in my patients, I was able to observe directly the *alternation of genital and cardiac excitation,* of sexual sensations in the genitals and of anxiety sensations in the cardiac region. As long as patients do not permit themselves to be aware of sexual excitation, they suffer from anxiety, which is ex-

perienced physically in the region of the heart and diaphragm. If, on the other hand, they permit themselves to
be aware of their sexual excitement, the anxiety constriction disappears and the genital organs become turgescent
(erection, moistening of the female genitals, etc.). In an
anxiety state, physical symptoms appear which are exactly
antithetical to those in sexual excitation. We find cold shiv-
ering, pallor, an urge to defecate and urinate, and perspiring.
There is an increase in heartbeat, with the occasional systolic contraction being skipped, and the mouth is dry. In
men, the penis shrinks; in women, the sex organs are completely dry (with sensations as in vaginismus). In the state
of sexual excitation, on the other hand, sensations of heat
are experienced (in women, especially in the area of the
genitals, neck, and throat), the genital organs are turgescent, secretion is abundant, and the heart beats normally or
it is in a state of diastolic expansion ("cardiac dilation").
In the region of the heart and diaphragm, sensations occur
which resemble those of anxiety but are also clearly distinct
from them. Patients speak of "tightness" or "constriction"
in anxiety and of "expansion" in pleasure. Such terms prove
to be very important, for, as will be seen, they directly
reflect an internal state. The organ sensations are expressed
in direct and correct language.

The antithesis of anxious and sexual excitation is also
evident in other states. Just as the genitals "shrink" in anxiety (due to vasoconstriction), so they expand, stretch,
and fill up in the state of sexual excitation. That is also
true of the genital glands. Pallor, especially in fright, con-
trasts with a light red coloration of the skin in sexual excitation. In fright, we are particularly conscious of the sudden
energetic emptying of the periphery, starting with the musculature of the extremities and experienced directly in a

sensation of paralysis. If, in a fright situation, reflex defensive behavior nevertheless occurs, the sensation of fright follows close behind. The sensation of paralysis of the motor apparatus follows the action; or the heartbeat stops for several seconds after a single, strong systole.

Thus, in both antithetical cases, excitation takes place in the vegetative life apparatus; but in sexual excitation the *parasympathetic* reaction, and in anxious excitation the *sympathetic* reaction, predominates. We can already note that the parasympathetic and sympathetic form a *unit* as a system, *but at the same time they can function in an antithetical relationship to each other.*

Parasympathetic   Sympathetic

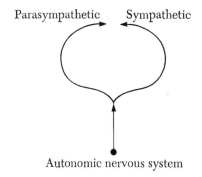

Autonomic nervous system

Just as, under certain conditions, they can function simultaneously as a unit—e.g., in fright, diarrhea and urination can occur suddenly, along with the sympathetic contraction of the peripheral vessels—so they can also inhibit each other, as when the sympathetic fibers of the stomach ganglion are deactivated and bleeding occurs in the intestinal mucous membranes. We know, too, that anxiety apprehension and sexual anticipation, despite the antithesis between them, are related, and that qualitatively similar sensations occur in both cases in the area of the heart and diaphragm and in the region of the coeliac ganglion. These sensations are very closely related to the aura of epileptics. Closer examination of epileptics reveals that the aura occurring before a seizure resembles pleasure anxiety, sometimes more that of pure anxiety, sometimes more of pure pleasure. In the latter, it is felt in the genital region.

On the basis of these facts, it is justified to assume that innervation and excitation of the vegetative system vary. When the body's *periphery* is excited, sexual sensation is generated; when the *center*, the area around the heart and diaphragm, is excited, anxiety is experienced. In this way, the idea of a *functional antithesis between body center and body periphery*, an idea which is gaining in fundamental importance, was added for the first time to the sex-economic theory of affect.

The view that pleasure (sexual excitation) and anxiety are two antithetical phenomena in the same nervous apparatus—i.e., the vegetative system—links up the fact, well known in the physiology of anxiety, that anxiety and vegetative excitation are functionally related. The only new aspect it introduces is that the vegetative system is also linked with the sexual function (as the antithesis of anxiety) and that an antithetical innervation of the vegetative apparatus is involved. On the basis of these observations and facts, we would now like to show that the system "sexuality–vegetative system–anxiety" is first of all functionally identical with the directions of flow of the blood and tissue fluid.

The Misch choline experiment

The physiological problem of anxiety has been approached from many angles. The link with the carbon-dioxide metabolism during shortness of breath, the anxiety attacks associated with angina pectoris, the feeling of constriction accompanying bronchial asthma, and similar pathologies, all pointed consistently toward a direct physiological manifestation of the anxiety affect. If research on the function of the orgasm has traced the anxiety problem from the complicated psychic phenomena of anxiety to the border of the realm of physiology, one would have expected physiology to supply the rest of the information, in the same way that "a tunnel dug from two directions meets in the middle." But this linkup did not happen, partly because the physiological study of nerves did not proceed beyond mechanical nerve-muscle experiments, which do not provide a theoretical overview, and partly because the only way in which access could be gained to the problem—namely, via the connection between anxiety and sexuality—was scorned by physiologists and blocked by traditional views of sexuality which had long been shown to be incorrect. It was all the more significant, then, that two analytically trained neurologists, Drs. Walter and Käthe Misch, inspired by the new problem of the function of the orgasm (1927), ventured to study the physiology of anxiety by means of pharmacological experiments.

They skillfully combined their therapeutic interest with theory. In their report "Die vegetative Genese der neurotischen Angst und ihre medikamentöse Beseitigung" (*Der Nervenarzt*, Vol. 5, 1932, No. 8), they note that Oppenheim and Hoche, in their major convention reports of 1910, had indicated the futility of all therapeutic attempts of a pharmacological and hydrotherapeutic kind. They started by examining the pure syndrome of anxiety neurosis; i.e., peripheral vasoconstriction, tachycardia, arterial hypertension, mydriasis, cessation of salivation, cold sweats, flaccidity of the muscles with tremors, diarrhea—all of which symptoms indicate a high degree of excitation of the vegetative system with a predominant reaction of the *sympathetic*. It was logical to assume that a drug which was able to dilate the peripheral vessels, slow the heart, lower the blood pressure, stimulate salivation, and improve tone of the striated muscles—that is, a preparation that has an essentially *parasympathetic* effect—ought to eliminate the anxiety syndrome. The choline preparations show themselves to be such drugs. According to the above-mentioned authors, they "fit the somatic anxiety syndrome like a key in a lock." The preparations are able "to eliminate immediately not only the somatic anxiety syndrome, but also the psychic anxiety experience." They administered 0.1 c.c. acetylcholine to patients intramuscularly, and within a few minutes observed improved circulation in the skin, a decrease in the tachycardia to nearly normal values, and the disappearance of the subjective physical symptoms. Simultaneously, the anxiety state, which could otherwise not be influenced, disappeared completely and gave way to a feeling of total well-being. An oral dose of choline preparations (4–6 tablets of Pacyl, 3 tablets of Hypotan daily) prevented any recurrence of the severe anxiety states.

Furthermore, it was evident that the more physical the anxiety effect, and the less the anxiety is anchored in the psyche (in compulsion neuroses, not much could be done), the greater is the choline effect. They attribute this essentially to the action of the choline, which is exactly the opposite of that of the sympathetic nervous system. The following is a table of the two syndromes, according to Misch:

	Anxiety syndrome	Choline effect
skin vessels	contracted	dilated
heart action	accelerated	slowed
blood pressure	increased	lowered
pupils	dilated	narrowed
salivation	decreased	increased
muscles	atonic	tonic

In contrast to the authors of this exquisite experiment, I prefer to lay more emphasis on its theoretical rather than its practical, therapeutic significance, because it seems to me more important to prevent anxiety than to treat it, although I by no means wish to underestimate the importance of therapy. But the more comprehensive question of the prophylaxis of neuroses, which in essence is *anxiety prophylaxis*, requires first a complete theoretical interpretation of this experiment. The latter confirmed the assumption I made in 1922–27, based on the psychoanalytic therapy of neuroses; namely, that the problem of the "somatic core of neurosis" is a pathological excitation state of the vegetative system.[*]

The two biophysical basic forms of psychic functions: "Toward the world"—"Away from the world"

If we now trace the antithesis of sexual excitation and anxiety by observing its psychic complications, and if we look for its manifestations in the "higher" psychic func-

[*] Cf. *Die Funktion des Orgasmus,* Int. Psychoan. Verlg., 1927. [Published in a revised version as *Genitality in the Theory and Therapy of Neurosis* (New York: Farrar, Straus and Giroux, 1980)—Ed.]

tions, we encounter first of all a wealth of mechanisms and functions which seemingly do not belong together. Only when they have been arranged according to genetic-theoretical criteria do we realize that we are forced to assume a *basic antithesis of vegetative life* if we want to understand the higher psychic antitheses. Psychoanalysis has distinguished between a number of pairs of opposites of psychic strivings, the first being that of *the individual and the outer world*. Libidinous interest directed toward the self is called *narcissistic libido* and that directed toward the world is called *object libido*. According to psychoanalysis, the latter is said to proceed out of the "narcissistic reservoir" of libidinous energy. Furthermore, psychoanalysis compares the way objects in the outside world are invested with interest with the way a unicellular organism stretches out its pseudopodia, which can be drawn in again. This "drawing in of libido," the removal of interest, is understood as a return to the "narcissistic state," as for example when falling asleep. Yet interest can at any time be directed once more out of the ego toward objects (e.g., awakening, falling in love, etc.). Object interest, then, can revert to narcissistic interest, which is its starting point. Thus, the antithesis "individual-outer world" is represented as an antithesis of narcissistic libido and object libido. Just as both form a unity, they can also contradict each other, as happens when the gratification of an object interest conflicts with a narcissistic interest in self-preservation. For example, the incestuous love of a little boy for his mother always comes into conflict with his narcissistic interest in his ego, in particular his genital organ. The renunciation of a drive and the repression of an impulse thus always originate in a narcissistic interest in self-preservation and, to start with, cause a withdrawal of the object interest.

If we pursue another antithesis, namely, that of destructive impulses and anxiety about carrying out the destruction, we would be inclined from the start to see this anxiety as deriving from the checked destructive impulse alone; for *every destructive impulse, when it is checked, produces anxiety.* But the question is whether the destructiveness is a primary impulse, as psychoanalytic theory contends, or a secondary phenomenon, as sex-economy hypothesizes. *Destructiveness is a biological reaction to the denial of sexual gratification.* Like sexual excitation, it strives "toward the world," and only its goal is different. The sexual impulse seeks to attain pleasure, while the destructive impulse seeks to eliminate a source of unpleasure in the outside world and to destroy the basis of the unpleasure. Thus, both sexuality and destructiveness have the same direction: toward the world; but their goals are decidedly opposed. If one loves and hates the same object simultaneously, the love impulse tends to curb the fulfillment of the hate impulse, and this itself tends to be transformed into a guilt feeling (as a compromise between love and hate for the same object). On the other hand, unrequited love can turn into hatred or can greatly increase already existing hatred. Sadism stems from the combination of sexuality and destructiveness. Perhaps the most apt way of expressing these phenomena is to say: *If one cannot move lovingly toward the world, one tries to destroy it.* Or to put it differently: *a destructive act is the substitute for unattainable gratification in love.* The antithesis common to both these impulses is *anxiety,* which can be seen as a *flight away from the world, a withdrawal into the ego.* This flight can be caused by an external obstacle to the gratification of a drive, or by an inner inhibition about approaching the outside world. In both cases, anxiety tends to develop, at least incipiently. Thus, the direction "toward the world" (sexually or destructively) is fundamentally opposed to the direction "away from the world." The latter exists at its most primitive biological level as a "crawling into one-self."* On a higher biological plane, this reaction is never lost; it is simply supplemented by a second, muscular re-action; namely, moving away from the source of unpleasure. As the ability to cope with the outside world develops fur-ther, the source of unpleasure or danger (destruction) is eliminated, and finally the external difficulties are intel-lectually foreseen and overcome (civilized precautions).

One can conclude from these functional relationships that the destructive aggression, which plays such a pre-dominant role in both social and individual existence, is a phylogenetically and also ontogenetically more recent func-tion than the two primary functions of "sexuality" and "anx-iety." We will see that this minor divergence from the views of Freud, who attempted to comprehend libido and de-structiveness as drives of equal biological depth, results in very far-reaching clinical-theoretical and sociological dif-ferences. Sex-economy thus denies the primary nature of the destructive drives and instead considers them to be phylogenetic derivatives of the functions of sexual denial, on the one hand, and of avoidance of anxiety on the other. This view can be supported in phylogenetic terms by the fact that the musculature—i.e., the destruction apparatus— develops out of the mesoderm of the gastrula, a secondary embryonic anlage, while the apparatus of the sexual and anxiety functions are already present in the unicellular organism.

---

* An extreme consequence of this anxiety function is the resignation and shrinking of the life apparatus in the cancer biopathy (cf. Reich, "The Carcinomatous Shrinking Biopathy," *International Journal of Sex-Economy and Orgone Research*, I/II, 1942). [Chapter V in *The Cancer Biopathy* (New York: Farrar, Straus and Giroux, 1973)—Ed.]

The fact that the inhibition of a destructive impulse produces anxiety in the same way as does inhibition of a sexual impulse, but that anxiety is avoided if the destructiveness is not simply curbed but turned against the self— i.e., if it becomes a self-destructive tendency—will one day be very important for gaining an understanding of the psychic apparatus. *I reject therefore the hypothesis of a primary self-destructive drive.* The development of anxiety is inversely related to masochistic self-destructive tendencies. That fact refutes the psychoanalysts who assume that anxiety is the expression of inner perceptions of self-destructive tendencies. The latter view is correct, provided we distinguish destructiveness which is merely inhibited from destructiveness which is turned against oneself.

Let us summarize our genetic view of the pairs of opposite drives:

Developmental stages of the anxiety reaction

Withdrawal into the self: protozoic reaction.
Flight, physical movement away from the object: metazoic reaction.
Destructiveness, destruction of sources of danger: metazoic reaction.
Civilized coping with existence: intellectual foresight, human-social reaction.

"Toward the world"	*"Away from the world"*
Sexuality	Sexual anxiety
Hatred	Fear of destruction
Destructiveness	Guilt feelings or self-destructiveness
Coping with tasks	Schizophrenic autism, catatonic stupor
Work performance, changing the world	Metaphysical idealism, religion

These are the psychological hypotheses which result from reducing complicated phenomena to simple biological antitheses. They coincide with the view that sexual excitation and anxiety are antithetically related in anxiety neurosis. Neither destructiveness nor self-destructive drives, neither muscular flight nor intellectual mastery of dangers are found in pure anxiety neurosis. Anxiety neurosis therefore seems an especially appropriate area in which to examine the problem of the border zone between the psychic and the physical.

TENDENCY TO ASSUME SPHERICAL FORM

When fleeing from the world, all living creatures have a tendency to assume a spherical form, or something similar to it if a fully developed skeletal structure is present. It is enough to mention a few typical examples here:

If one touches the feelers of a snail with a blade of grass, it first draws in its feelers and remains otherwise immobile. After a pause, it extends its feelers again slowly. If touched once more, it pulls them in more quickly than before and also begins to withdraw its body into its shell.

At rest and when making simple movements, the earthworm is stretched out and "relaxed." If one touches the front end, it retracts this part, which grows shorter and fatter; or the worm rolls itself up. Where an animal has lost the ability to withdraw into itself, when it is no longer possible for it to change from the elongate to the spherical form, we find that the body rolls up, into an illusory sphere, so to speak. This is what happens when a hedgehog is threatened; its limbs are drawn up to the body, the back is rounded, the head is brought close to the legs. One is automatically reminded of the position of the embryo.

One can observe this withdrawal best of all in the

amoeba. The pseudopodia, which previously gave the cell a polymorphous appearance, disappear; surface unevenness smooths out, and the cell takes on more and more the form of a sphere. The spherical form also predominates before division and after copulation.

When multicellular creatures "start" with fright, it is undoubtedly the same kind of phenomenon in principle. This action can by no means be interpreted as "deliberate," as if it were based on the deduction that a smaller surface area is more difficult to attack. Such a superficially rationalistic interpretation of the process only brings us closer to theology, but otherwise does not take us one step further. We can explain this phenomenon in another way.

The spherical shape, whether it is attained by drawing in protruding organs (pseudopodia, feelers in the snail, etc.), or by arching the spine and drawing in the head and extremities, is expressive of the function "away from the world." In contrast, the stretching of the body, the putting forth or extension of the extremities and the head, the "expansion away from the body center," indicates the function "toward the world." We will come across the logical continuation of this function again later, in the merging of two organisms. First, however, we must examine some facts which reveal the functions described above in their primary vegetative form.

THE PRIMARY VEGETATIVE FORM OF THE ANTITHESIS BETWEEN SEXUALITY AND ANXIETY

The flow of body fluids and psychic "tendency" in the organism

Let us summarize the foregoing facts in order to link up with what follows. In the anxiety state, the body fluid (blood and other liquids) flows away from the periphery. In a state of sexual excitation, the opposite takes place. There is increased turgor of the peripheral tissues; the skin and mucous membranes become engorged with blood; and secretions from the salivary and genital glands increase.

Dilation of the peripheral vessels *dissipates* anxiety (effect of choline and of alcohol). Impeding of sexual motility and of peripheral turgor produces anxiety (adrenalin effect, sexual inhibition).

Regardless of these physiological facts, we are obliged to assume that, in the psychic apparatus, emotional interest is directed on the one hand "toward the world" and on the other "away from the world."

In the biological world, we generally find two opposite directions or functions resulting either in the spherical form or in its opposite; namely extension and expansion.

We notice that in every case the direction of flow of the fluids is the same as that of the psychic or, rather, biological direction of function. Tendencies toward the world —expansion, dissipation of anxiety, etc.—go together with *centrifugal* flow. Tendencies away from the world—adoption of a spherical form, generation of anxiety, etc.—go together with *centripetal* flow. What we now have to find out is whether this is a coincidental concurrence or a previously overlooked *fundamental* law of life. This would be of the greatest importance for our theory of the functional identity of psychic and physical functions. First, we will briefly review a few elementary facts that will enable us to comprehend clearly a series of otherwise incomprehensible interrelations between physical and psychic functions.

In unicellular organisms and those multicellular organisms that have not developed a blood system, plasma has been found to move in certain ways that correlate with primitive life functions. In plant cells, plasma rotates and circulates. These movements respond promptly to electrical stimuli. For example, weak electrical stimuli retard the plasma movement, while stronger ones bring it to a complete standstill.

The phenomenon of plasmatic movement, both spontaneous and when modified by electrical stimuli, is seen most clearly in *amoebae*. Corpuscular elements in their protoplasm prove to be spherical vesicles filled with fluid.* The "contractile vacuole" is just such a spherical fluid-filled vesicle, which collapses from time to time, thereby emptying out the liquid it contains. According to Max Hartmann, the movement of amoebae depends directly on plasma flow. When the amoeba moves forward, plasma flows from the center to the periphery (thus creating the pseudopodium) and then back along the sides of the amoeba body. If the amoeba is touched, the plasma flow reverses itself; i.e., plasma flows from the pseudopodium back into the center. This is how the pseudopodia are retracted. If the amoeba has put out several pseudopodia and if by chance it touches something solid, the plasma flows in the direction of the pseudopodium which is in contact with the solid body, while the other pseudopodia are retracted by the plasma being emptied out. When the organism is feeding, the plasma always flows in a peripheral direction. It reacts negatively, moving away, in response to chemical, thermal, electrical, and photic stimuli. According to the observations of Rhumbler, Engelmann,

---

* [1945] These vesicles are nothing other than the "bions" or "orgone energy vesicles," discovered in 1936, which make up all living tissues.

Harrington, Davenport, et al., amoebae leave off feeding when suddenly exposed to light; they even release the particles they have swallowed, and then contract. They flow freely under red light, but are inhibited by blue light, though the amoeba will always move in the direction of a steady source of light. The substructure of the amoeba's vital activity system is nothing more than a *vegetative flow of plasma.*

Let us summarize the most important biological findings about this plasma flow and its associated structural form. First of all, we must remember that, according to Rhumbler, in centrifugal plasma flow, the watery plasma mass of the cell body (endoplasm) changes into the viscous plasma of the periphery (ectoplasm). In centripetal (also called "spherogenic")—i.e., reverse—flow, the viscous ectoplasm changes back to watery endoplasm. The observation would seem to corroborate F. Kraus's assumption that fundamental organic movements involve hydration or dehydration of a colloidal substance; i.e., a change in the density of the substance by means of a change in its water content.

According to Max Hartmann, most phenomena of pseudopodal movement demonstrate the predominantly liquid state of protoplasm. The movement itself, according to existing studies, is a result of the constant *alternation of expansion and contraction,* which is the same whether it occurs in the plasma of a unicellular organism or in the muscles of a multicellular organism. Here again, *contraction* (tendency to become spherical) and *expansion* (tendency to become elongated) alternate. We consider it important that, according to Hofer and Gruber, even bodies of protoplasm whose nuclei have been removed form pseudopodia for days afterwards.

There is uniform agreement today about the well-known view, which was first put forward by Buetschli, Berthold, and Quincke, that pseudopodal movement can be attributed to the hydromechanical laws of surface tension.* At the interface between two immiscible fluids (e.g., oil and water, salt electrolyte and colloidal electrolyte), surface tensions and surface energies come into play, and the same thing happens in plasma. These energies include, first, *internal pressure,* which strives to enlarge the surface from the center, and, second, *surface tension,* which acts on the center from the periphery (and furthermore acts tangentially to the curvature of the surface). The pressure of the volume energy is proportional to the surface tension and inversely proportional to the radius. If the surface tension of the surrounding medium is less than that of the drop of plasma, the surface tension of the latter will prevail and bring about the spherical form (state of equilibrium). It is assumed that a pseudopodium is formed whenever the surface tension at any point on the surface decreases *for any reason.* This view does not take in the essential aspect of the process, for if it did, the movement would be merely passive. In reality, when plasma begins to flow, it suggests that there is a force acting from within. It is tempting to jump to premature vitalistic conclusions, which we have every reason to avoid. Of course, the effect of internal pressure alone is not enough to explain the endogenous tendency to expand, because we would then have to explain why an inorganic drop does *not* move, even though it, too, has internal pressure. *There must be something in addition to me-*

---

* [1945] When the biological energy was discovered, this mechanistic interpretation of protoplasmic movement was replaced by the *functional* explanation of *expansion* and *contraction.* These functions also proved to be specific functions of orgone energy in the non-living realm.

*chanical tension which produces movement in that which is
alive.**

In this regard, the model tests conducted by Buetschli
to imitate the plasma flow in the amoeba are very important. If we bring oil drops, potassium carbonate, and
water drops together for a while, we get emulsified drop-
lets of oil, which generally begin to flow without much
change of shape after they have been washed out with
water. If we substitute diluted glycerine for the water, and
if we then squeeze the oil drops under a cover glass, they
not only flow about but form polymorphous processes. We
see the same *centrifugal* axial flows and return flows along
the periphery as in the amoeba when it is forming pseudopodia. And, as in the amoeba, increasing the temperature
will speed up the formation of artificial pseudopodia in the
oil drop as well.

Hartmann is certain that surface energy is the principle
behind the movement in the formation of artificial pseudopodia, but he feels that despite many hypotheses, no one
has explained why the surface tension decreases or increases. According to a hypothesis put forward by Jensen,
assimilation is said to produce a decrease, and dissimilation
an increase, in surface tension; i.e., in the first case, expansion, and in the second, contraction. The essence of this
process is claimed to be the increase in the number of
molecules during dissimilation (catabolism) and the decrease in the number of molecules (anabolism) during assimilation.

Whatever the case, we have no reason to doubt that *in
the two opposite directions of plasma flow in the unicellular*

* [1945] The force involved is in all cases the *internal* expansion impulse
of the organismic orgone. This text of 1934 raised a basic question about
living matter, which was an important signpost pointing the way to the
discovery of orgone energy.

*organism we have the prototype of the two psychic currents
we have postulated; namely, the "sexual" toward the world
and the "anxious" away from the world.*

Some problems branch off at this point, but I can only
hint at them here, and with one exception will not pursue
them further in this study. First of all, it is clear that the
leap from the passive movement of the oil drop, produced
by mechanical change in surface tension, to the active,
endogenous flow of plasma in the unicellular organism contains the riddle of the formation of organic from inorganic
matter.* Furthermore, the problem of surface tension
touches on the question of cell division, which will concern
us elsewhere.

Finally, the question arises, what bridges lead from the
two directions of plasma flow to the complicated phenomena of sexuality and anxiety? For only by proving the
continuum of the function can we support our fundamental
assumption that sexuality and anxiety are antithetical primary functions of all living matter.

We know that in the living system a functional antithesis exists between center and periphery. Anxiety is to be
understood fundamentally as a central stasis of fluid (in
psychological terms, central excitation), and pleasure in
general, as well as sexual pleasure in particular, is to be
seen as a peripheral expansion of body fluids (in psychological terms, peripheral excitation). In the former, there
is simultaneously a draining of fluid from the periphery,
and central excitation; in the latter, there is central relaxation and peripheral excitation. In an anxiety state, tension
is felt centrally (constriction); in sexual tension, it is felt
peripherally (e.g., in the erection of the genitals). To make

* [1945] This view was fully confirmed in 1936 when contractile bions
were produced experimentally from non-living matter.

the point more clearly, let me mention two drugs, adrenalin and alcohol, which have antithetical effects on the vascular system. Adrenalin produces anxiety in a direct physiological way; alcohol relieves constriction and anxiety, just as choline does, by dilating the peripheral vessels. Now, it is important to understand more precisely the relationships of the vegetative apparatus to the vascular apparatus, for a concrete functional link exists here both with the anxiety affect and with sexual excitation.

KRAUS'S "FLUID THEORY OF LIFE"

Let us turn to the "fluid theory of life" of F. Kraus, which appears to do what we would expect of a physiological theory of the autonomic nervous system: it synthesizes the phenomena and functions of living matter into one unified fundamental concept. Some people object that it is dangerous to build on this theory, because it is itself controversial. I would refute this by pointing out that there are certain criteria governing the applicability and correctness of a theory which make judgment possible. Theories usually are highly controversial. We know how seldom new discoveries find favor with scientists in general and with colleagues in particular. We cannot expect too much from the much-lauded objectivity of scientific criticism. Direct experience of the scientific scene teaches us how criticism within the various disiplines is greatly swayed by personal inclinations, traditional thinking, and ties of friendship. It is usually impossible to form for oneself an expert opinion about new theories from unfamiliar special fields. It seems dangerous to base one's trust solely on the plausibility of a new idea, for what is plausible is not always correct, and because all too often one is tempted to yield to one's own expectations and inclinations. When, however, workers in various disciplines, independent of one another, without being aware of the consequences of their research and without any expectation that their research will coincide, nevertheless converge more and more on a certain point, when they develop similar or even identical views about this point of convergence, and when, finally, certain problems can be solved only by considering two or three autonomous views without resorting to any others, then there is no doubt that these theories, and not the heuristically worthless, isolated ones, are more probably correct.

When it is found, then, that certain discoveries made independently of one another by the biologist Hartmann, the internist Kraus, and the psychologist Freud converge in a certain direction, when, finally, sex-economic research on the function of the orgasm and its relation to the vegetative nervous system led me in the same direction, when these views confirm my own findings and synthesize them into a unified construct of psychophysical relationships, no doubts voiced from whatever quarter about any of these other views should be permitted to stop me from evaluating them, as long as the critics have nothing better or more plausible to put in their place.

In presenting Kraus's theory, I will confine myself to the fundamental aspects which are indispensable for an understanding of our problem. But I would recommend that every reader who wishes to penetrate deeper into the subject study Kraus's work "Allgemeine und spezielle Pathologie der Person," *Klinische Syzygiologie* (Thieme, 1926).

In the plasma flow of the amoeba we encounter in principle the same two opposite directions with which we were concerned in connection with the problem of the antithesis of sexuality and anxiety; namely, a flow "toward the world" and a flow "away from the world." The psychic tendencies and physiological flow directions are closely related to one another in a manner which we do not yet understand.

Some of Kraus's basic concepts actually meet our own sex-economic views halfway. Kraus proceeds from the basic fact that living matter is essentially colloidal in structure. Colloids are solutions of matter in water which do not break down into molecules but merely into largish particles. There are many gradations from a colloidal solution to a saline solution. As a result, the rigid boundary between the living and the non-living world, which has long been defended, becomes blurred. To start with, the colloidal solution is distinguished from the saline solution in that it does not pass through membranes. It has in common with saline solution the fact that it is an electrolyte. Kraus sees the biosystem as an excitation system, a "relay-like triggering mechanism," an apparatus operated by charge (i.e., storage of work) and discharge, which is based entirely on energized interfaces. Of these interfaces, the crucial ones are those between a salt electrolyte and a colloidal electrolyte. The life process is characterized by deoxidization, the production of carbon dioxide, and the generation of electrical energy at the interfaces. The saline solution is an indispensable factor of life, long before blood develops. Kraus believes that the transportation and distribution of matter are far more important for the reproduction of the life process than metabolism, which is the purely chemical conversion of the ingested matter itself. The life process can be defined as an independent vegetative flow, and essentially as a convection of fluids. We have to distinguish between the mechanical convection of the fluid—as, for example, in blood circulation and lymph circulation—the directional movement of dietary fluids, and finally, most importantly, the microscopic movement of protoplasm. The general movement of fluid in the organism has a far more significant function to perform than merely providing nutrients for the various areas. Instead, its function is ensured only when an infinite number of interfaces form between fluids of differing densities and composition, thereby creating electrical potential. To the electrically charged interfaces are added the purely mechanical surface tensions which act as a vectorial factor. *The biosystem is powered by the equalization of the interface potentials.** Surfaces of different potential act in exactly the same way as electrolytic systems, in which they are the electrodes. The organic membranes and the interface between the salt electrolyte and the colloidal electrolyte are the chief interfaces. In order for electric current to flow, it is not only necessary for the membranes (electrodes) to be charged, but they must also be connected. This connection is made by the body fluids, which act as an electrolyte, but are also *more* than that. The biosystem not only charges itself with electrical energy but also equalizes these potentials and forms currents between and within the inner membranes through the conducting substance of the body itself. Thus, a conducting connection applied from the outside for experimental purposes would only be a shunt. Electricity arises from the movements of fluid (according to Kraus, free electrical charges wander about in the capillaries). The differences in potential in question, which bring about equalization, are located at the interface between moving and stationary fluids. In the process of equalization, the electrical energy is converted to mechanical energy. This "fluid theory of

---

* [1945] (Correction to Kraus's view): The origin of the gradient of the electrical potential is in itself a problem. The actual motor of that which is alive is orgone energy. We still do not know how or why electrical motor forces form at the membranes from the body orgone.

life," however, can be maintained only if the protoplasmic events can be correlated with the laws governing colloidal solutions in general.

Let us say a few more words about Kraus's concept. Unquestionably, it describes (without naming) the same thing which I regard as the basis of the orgasm: the conversion of mechanical tension into electrical charge *(tension-charge process)* and the conversion of electrical discharge into mechanical relaxation *(discharge-relaxation process). Thus, the orgasm would be the potentiated special case of vegetative flow in general.*

If one isolates the lower half of the pulvinus in a mimosa and stimulates it, for example, thermally, the leaf will fall off; galvanic negativity is obtained. At the same time, it is seen that water is expelled from the node and there is a corresponding decrease in turgor. If one stimulates the upper half, however, the leaf stretches out. Even if one prevents the mechanical reaction, the electrical reaction still takes place. If, when one immerses the twig in water, the pulvinus becomes excessively turgid—i.e., erect—the leaf will not fall, because it is difficult to expel the water. All plants and plant organs react electrically.

Let us recapitulate that the uptake of water goes together with an increase in turgescence and expansion ("erection"), and the expulsion of water occurs along with abscission of the leaf and a decrease in turgescence. I will discuss elsewhere the meaning of this experiment from the point of view of understanding the erection and shrinking of the penis. In principle, the processes are functionally identical.

In the hair cells of *Cucurbita pepo*, which possesses a circulating plasma, Velten observed that the plasma was composed of a rather dark, granular, probably colloid-rich substance, and a lighter, more aqueous, hyaline substance.

According to Kraus, the two together form what he calls the "critical fluid mixture," which is a fundamental characteristic of living matter. Microscopic observation of the behavior of such "critical fluid mixtures" in living matter reveals that, initially, the granules are in a quiescent state. If granules from the denser stratum enter the thinner, less viscous, more aqueous stratum, they exhibit lively Brownian movement.* If a weak induction current passes through the cell, a large number of granules start to undergo molecular movement; the flow slows down. If a stronger current is applied, swellings appear in various places. The plasma thread then either forms spherical processes or it puts out fine threads. If the stimulation is interrupted, the latter are retracted again and regular plasma flow continues. The swellings are caused by water uptake from the more aqueous layer of plasma. The point can be reached where the swollen part separates off from the plasma thread by constriction and swims around freely in the cell liquid.

All organic bodies exhibit a steady flow of water. The most essential functions of the water flow are: metabolism to promote tissue growth as well as to eliminate solid matter, metabolic wastes, and salts; the evaporation of water from the skin and lung; the replacement of water by the intake of food and drink, etc. On average, the water content of the body remains the same. According to Kraus, it amounts to 70% water in adults. In the blood it is 80%, in the skin 70%, and in the brain 75%, etc. We have already mentioned that plasma movement is the most important feature. Stern† discovered that plasma movements react to weak electrical stimuli by slowing down, and to stronger stimuli by coming to a standstill. Essentially, the

---

* [1945] Bion research has explained this movement as resulting from the function of orgonotic forces of attraction and repulsion.

† *Elektrophysiologie der Pflanze*, Springer, 1924.

changes that occur in the plasma when stimuli are applied are as follows: the movement of the plasma accelerates and slows down, the plasma swells and shrinks, expands and contracts; substances become mixed or segregated, precipitate out or enter into solution; granules appear and disappear; the viscosity also varies (Kraus). The stimuli (electric as well as others) cause shifts in distribution and changes in concentration of the ions present in the medium, the cell fluid, and in the plasma.

A. W. Greeley was the first to test experimentally the general notion that the effects of electrical current on cells are attributable to changes in the ion concentration and their effect on the colloidal system. He found that acids and salts with multivalent cations thicken the plasma, while alkalies and salts with multivalent anions make it fluid. Kraus draws a fundamental conclusion from this: *If any stimulus impinging on the protoplasmic substance threatens the stability of the colloidal substance, this is because a shift occurs in the complexes of the colloidal and inorganic electrolytes of the body. As a result, changes occur in the energy potentials at the surface of the membranes, and this in turn promotes new electrical discharges. Since organisms are continuously exposed to external and internal stimuli, we can see that the fundamental characteristic of living substance is represented by the change in energy potentials and by the equalization of changes that have already taken place. All this happens in the form of alternations between charge and discharge, tension and relaxation.*

---

* [1945] In the meantime, the discovery of the orgone has enabled us to make an important correction here: electrical processes can be stimuli or accompanying phenomena of the life functions. They can change, disrupt, or promote the orgonotic life processes, *but they cannot bring them about.*

We can raise a basic question at this point. Charge and discharge, tension and relaxation, are physical processes which govern inorganic nature as well. Living matter is distinguished from inorganic matter first of all by the independent alternation of these functions. *What brings about this independence?* Investigation of the orgastic function, in which we see an elementary life process, taught us that tension and charge, discharge and relaxation, are functionally related in a certain way. Mechanical tension leads to an electrical charge, and electrical discharge leads to mechanical relaxation, which then is transformed again into mechanical tension, and so on. Is this specific link between mechanics and electricity perhaps the distinguishing characteristic of living matter? We will return often to this question.

The basic mechanism of the psychic apparatus is a system of alternating tension and relaxation. Our concept of drive stands and falls on the idea that psychic events are a matter of tension and relaxation, charge and discharge of energy. That would not mean much if it were only an analogy. But there is more to it: the events and processes are homologous, or identical.

We cannot fully reproduce here the extensive and illuminating proof which Kraus provides to help the reader understand his train of thought. Nor is it important in our context to critically analyze his proofs. We could not do so, in any case. Assuming that his fundamental concept is correct—i.e., that the organ system (organic interfaces, colloid/salt electrolyte system, the biosystem as an electrical relay apparatus, etc.) is driven by vegetative flow of fluid—then Kraus's experiments on living specimens, which we will mention now, acquire enormous importance for us. We will summarize them in brief. They are based on a concept that Kraus puts as follows: "There is no individual life process which does not somehow—either directly or indirectly, wholly or in part—ultimately stem from ion activity. As in the case of oxygen, there is no substitute for electrolytes. Most conditions of illness, whether functional or so-called organic illnesses, are ultimately explained by vegetative flow."

POTASSIUM AND CALCIUM IONS AND THE VEGETATIVE FUNCTION

Voluntary muscle innervation is associated with the animal part of man; the involuntary unconscious innervation of smooth muscles and glands, and the fluid flow, are associated with the vegetative functions (heart, intestine, sexual organs, etc.). Yet the vegetative function is carried over into the voluntary functions; for example, in the form of muscle tonus as a result of continuous vegetative innervation. In organisms with brains, the vegetative system is represented by a special neural organization, in association with the sympathetic and parasympathetic ganglia. The question now arises: *Is there a system or something similar in living creatures without a developed vegetative apparatus that performs those functions which we later find are carried out by the vegetative system;* i.e., peristalsis, circulation, tonus, and turgor? In metazoa without a bony support structure, we find that neural ganglia have already developed. In the unicellular organism and in multicellular organisms up to a certain stage of development, no nervous system forms. *What, then, fulfills its function?* That is to say, what is the morphological forerunner of the vegetative system? Such wholly non-speculative questions force themselves upon us when we proceed from the processes of sexuality to the functional problems of living matter in general.

Physiology has long been concerned with the question of the specific effect of ions on the colloidal system; they represent the fundamental substance of life. If chemical substances exist which can (1) *strengthen* or *weaken* the effects of vegetative innervation; (2) *replace* these effects; (3) *complement* or *neutralize* each other's effect; and, finally, (4) are a specific component of protoplasm, as for example lecithin-cholesterol, then one is entitled to assume that these inorganic substances fulfill the later functions of the vegetative apparatus *before* it has developed; even perhaps that this apparatus is an organized, ongoing development of simple chemical processes. Here the experimental work of Kraus, Zondek, Dresel inter al., if they are fundamentally correct, is of great pioneering importance.

As regards the hydration or dehydration of the tissues (which, as we know, is the basic function of living matter), Kraus's experiments led him to conclude that the effects of nerves, toxins, and electrolytes are interchangeable in the biological system. Organic tissues are a combination of membranes and fluids. The membranes are complexes of protein, phosphatides, and sterols, together with the colloids, especially lecithin and cholesterol. Salt electrolytes vary in form and composition. To be chemically effective as stimulant substances, the salts must exist in dissolved, ionized form. The cations—sodium, potassium, calcium, magnesium, and iron—and the anions—chlorine, phosphorus, SO_3, iodine, and CO_2—are especially effective. These salt electrolytes retard or accelerate water movement, especially the uptake or discharge of water by the tissues. Since swelling and shrinking are directly related to the variations in surface tension, they are of fundamental importance for the biopsychic problem of tension and relaxation.

Zondek first showed that *potassium* (K), like sodium, has a diastolic—i.e., relaxing—periphery-expanding effect on a frog's heart, while *calcium* (Ca) has a systolic—i.e., constricting—central tension-producing effect. It is essentially a matter of fluid movements: one ion takes water toward the heart, the other removes it. Kraus and Zondek were able to observe the water movement directly in Straub's specimen and were also able to deduce it from the curve of the action currents. In connection with other experiments, *the parasympathetic system was seen to act like an addition of potassium* to the nutrient liquid of a muscle preparation, while *the sympathetic system, on the other hand, acts like an addition of calcium.*

Kraus comes to the totally logical conclusion that nerves and muscles are not independent structures, but rather that the nervous and muscular systems form a "syzygy," an interacting unit. In particular, the "vegetative nerve apparatus, as a protoplasmic link . . . produces connections between the membranes of various organs." As a coherent agglomeration of plasma, the nervous system is subject to the laws of colloidal electrolytes. Since antithetically acting groups of potassium and calcium ions are always present in such electrolytes, *the vegetative nervous system merely carries on, in an organized manner, a function which already exists in principle in animals without nervous systems;* i.e., the function of plasma movement, hydration and dehydration, contraction and expansion, tension and relaxation brought about by the ions of the salt electrolytes. It is important to note that cholesterol and lecithin, which are always present in the organic colloid, behave like calcium and the sympathetic system or like potassium and the parasympathetic system, respectively. The antagonism between lecithin and cholesterol is expressed by the fact that lecithin is a *hydrophilic* colloid which promotes water uptake, while cholesterol is a *hydrophobic* colloid which expels water. Dresel uses a lecithin-cholesterol mixture as a physiological model to test the effects of salt electrolytes on colloidal substances. If under certain conditions (given an approximately physiological concentration and a corresponding molecular composition of the electrolytes), potassium chloride or calcium chloride is added to such a mixture, the ion antagonism manifests itself in the sense that the potassium chloride *increases* and the calcium chloride *lowers* the surface tension of the lecithin-cholesterol mixture. Alkalies behave like potassium and acids like calcium. This is important for the understanding of certain organ-neurotic* phenomena.

A lecithin-Ringer's solution brings about a *diastolic* standstill in a frog's heart (Straub's experiment); i.e., a *parasympathetic* effect. A cholesterol-Ringer's solution brings about a *systolic* standstill; i.e., a *sympathetic* effect. *However, this effect on the heart muscle is the opposite of that on the peripheral muscles.* Potassium causes the peripheral muscles to go into tonic contraction or it heightens the effect of an electrical stimulus. Calcium, on the other hand, reduces the effect of an electrical stimulus and makes the muscles flaccid. This antithesis in the effect of the electrolytes on the heart muscle and on peripheral muscles, which Kraus does not explain further, is of central importance for our study. *It shows us directly the antithesis between the central heart function and the peripheral function of the muscular effector.* Here, too, Ca and K behave just like the sympathetic and parasympathetic systems. The parasympathetic innervation increases the tonus of the periph-

* [1945] That is, biopathic.

eral smooth and striated muscles, while the sympathetic innervation lowers it, just like the effect of K and Ca in the frog experiment. On the other hand, the parasympathetic system (N. depressor) retards the heart muscle to the point of *diastolic* standstill, whereas the sympathetic system (N. accelerans) has the opposite, namely, systolic, effect on the heart, which is the same as that on the peripheral muscles; that is to say, it increases tonus and activity and with overstimulation brings the heart to a *systolic* standstill. In addition, the parasympathetic effect can be reduced or even stopped by adding Ca; or it can be intensified by adding K. The sympathetic effect on the muscles can be stopped by adding K. This is further proof of the functional identity of the vegetative nervous system and certain groups of antagonistic ions. The stimulative effect of digitalis on the heart can be canceled out by K and supported by Ca, since K paralyzes heart function and Ca promotes it. A predominance of Ca in the tissues produces H-ion dissociation; a predominance of K produces OH-ion dissociation. A predominance of H ions means the death of the tissue. It may be very important for the understanding of vegetative life that, according to Kraus, K (i.e., the *hydrophilic* ion) predominates in the epithelium, while Ca (i.e., the *hydrophobic,* water-removing ion) predominates in the connective tissue. K also predominates during growth and Ca during maturity.* Cancerous tissues are said to contain large amounts of K and Ca, which might perhaps explain the tendency of the tissue cells to multiply in an uncontrolled manner (excess of K). Such findings permit the hypothesis that we must look for the life-promoting effects in the K ion group and the destructive

---

* [1945] This agrees fully with the preponderance of the *contraction function* in old age and in the shrinking biopathy, which underlies cancer.

effects in the Ca group.* The tonus of the musculature, according to Kraus, is essentially not an expression of some mysterious nerve fluid, but instead a state of plasmatic *electrolytic turgor*, an expression of the saturation tension of the muscle. According to this view, growth and increase in strength must be based on conditions under which more is gained than consumed in the process of dynamogenesis.

The parasympathetic system has an expanding effect on the peripheral vascular system and increases the surface tension; the sympathetic system has a constricting effect and lowers the surface tension. This antagonistic innervation prevails also in glands like the submaxillary; and

---

* Is the psychoanalytic hypothesis of a death instinct confirmed by this physiological basis of anxiety? Someone who believes this might say: if the accumulation of the K-ion group effect represents the sexual function, the Ca-ion group effect would be the death function, the dying off of the tissues. I would counter this with the same argument that I used in my investigation of character, and I would add one further argument: the K-ion concentration is felt subjectively as instinctual urge; the Ca-ion concentration, on the other hand, is not experienced as a drive, which would correspond to a death *wish*, but rather as *anxiety*. The death instinct is not "mute," but instead what is called the death instinct, namely the *retraction* of life energy, manifests itself clearly as anxiety. This thought takes us a step further. It is correct that the Ca group produces the same phenomena that we observe in a dying person (contraction of the peripheral vessels, pallor, anxiety, tremors, etc.). But these are only *objectively* given; they are not desired subjectively, like the K-ion effects. It is also correct that the Ca-ion group functions to further and accelerate aging and dying. Yet we would be wrong not to remember that this is a consequence of the impeding of *sexual* functions and that in the form of anxiety the organism *defends* itself against the increase of internal tension. *Finally, if chronic anxiety processes were to accelerate dying, it would not prove the existence of a death instinct, but rather of the anti-life effect of sexual inhibition, because the suppression of the parasympathetic function enhances the sympathetic function;* i.e., the processes of drying out, becoming enervated, and "crawling back into the self"—in short, the abatement of all life functions. Thus, we cannot find any arguments here in favor of the theory of a death instinct which would offer a defense of the life-inhibiting effects of society and disease.

according to an experiment carried out by Claude Bernard, the sympathetic system produces a scant amount of viscous (Ca = hydrophobic) mucus while the parasympathetic system generates a more copious and fluid mucus. Studies of secretion revealed that the increased pressure of the parenchyma of the gland is brought about by the parasympathetic influence, more precisely by the dilation of the tissues and by increased turgor. According to Kraus, the accelerated blood flow is more the result and not just the cause of this. According to an experiment conducted by Bernard, transection of the sympathetic nerve in the neck increases the vitality of the tissues by eliminating the sympathetic suppression of the parasympathetic effect.

THE ANTITHESIS OF CENTER AND PERIPHERY

Let me first of all present a synopsis of the functions of the parasympathetic and sympathetic, which together may be called the vegetative (autonomic) nervous system.*

Functioning of the autonomic nervous system

Sympathetic Effect	Organ	Parasympathetic Effect
Inhibition of the m. sphincter pupillae: *dilated pupils*	Musculature of the iris	Stimulation of the m. sphincter pupillae: *narrowing of the pupils*
Inhibition of the lachrymal glands: "dry eyes." Depression	Lachrymal glands	Stimulation of the lachrymal glands: "glowing eyes." Joy

* This synopsis is based on one appearing in Müller's handbook *Lebensnerven und Lebenstriebe* (3rd ed., Springer, 1931).—Ed.

Sympathetic Effect	Organ	Parasympathetic Effect
Inhibition of the salivary glands: "parched mouth"	Salivary glands	Stimulation and increased secretion of the salivary glands: "making mouth water"
Stimulation of the sweat glands in face and body: "skin is moist and cold"	Sweat glands	Inhibition of the sweat glands in face and body: "skin is dry"
Contraction of the arteries: "cold sweat," pallor, anxiety	Arteries	Dilatation of the arteries: "freshness" and flushing of skin, increased turgor without perspiration
Musculature of hair follicle is stimulated: hair bristles, "goose pimples," chills	Arrectores pilorum	Inhibition of arrectores pilorum: skin becomes smooth and warm
Inhibition of the contractive musculature: bronchi are relaxed	Bronchial musculature	Stimulates the contraction of the bronchial musculature: bronchi are narrowed
Stimulates cardiac action: palpitation, rapid heartbeat	Heart	Slows cardiac action: quiet heart, slower pulse
Inhibits peristalsis: reduces secretion of digestive glands	Digestive tract from esophagus to rectum, liver, pancreas, kidneys, all digestive glands	Stimulates peristalsis: increases secretion of digestive glands

Sympathetic Effect	Organ	Parasympathetic Effect
Increases adrenal secretion: anxiety reaction	Suprarenal gland	Reduces adrenal secretion: pleasure reaction
Inhibits musculature of the bladder, stimulates urinary sphincter: inhibits micturition	Urinary bladder	Stimulates musculature of the bladder, inhibits the sphincter: stimulates micturition
Tightening of the smooth musculature, reduces secretion of all glands, decrease of blood supply, dry vagina: reduction of sexual feeling	Female sex organs	Relaxation of the smooth musculature, stimulates all gland functions, increases blood flow, moist vagina: increase of sexual feeling
Tightening of the smooth musculature of the scrotum, reduction of gland functions, decrease of blood supply, flaccid penis: "diminished sexual desire"	Male sex organs	Relaxation of the smooth musculature of the scrotum, increases all secretions, increases blood flow, erection: "intensified sexual desire"

In this synopsis, we see differences in the respective innervation of the various organs. Sometimes it is the parasympathetic and at others the sympathetic that stimulates the muscles. The intestinal and stomach muscles, for example, are stimulated by the parasympathetic and inhibited by the sympathetic, whereas the innervation is just the reverse for the heart. While the sympathetic in general makes the smooth muscles flaccid, it contracts the muscles of the peripheral vessels, thus constricting them. It is striking that the sympathetic inhibits the salivary gland, while it stimulates the suprarenal gland, thereby promoting the secretion of adrenalin. The parasympathetic has the opposite effect. It is especially noteworthy that in one and the same organ—for example, the bladder—the sympathetic *stimulates* the muscle which *impedes* the flow of urine, but renders flaccid the muscle which *expels* the urine. The parasympathetic has the opposite effect. In other examples, the penis becomes flaccid when stimulated sympathetically; the smooth musculature of the scrotum becomes tense. Again, the parasympathetic has an opposite effect: erection of the penis; relaxation of the scrotal musculature. The smooth muscle of the iris is inhibited when sympathetically stimulated (dilation) and constricted when parasympathetically stimulated.

The laws of innervation seem to be arbitrary. As far as I have determined from the available literature, physiology has formed no opinion about the matter. We must assume that this "lack of order" in innervation is only apparent, and that it nonetheless actually follows a certain lawfulness. Apart from the antithesis of parasympathetic and sympathetic organ innervation, there is a *functional unity* in the innervation of each of the two systems, which can be understood only by considering the *overall function* of the organism. The following is a comparison based on this overall function:

Vegetative Group	General Effect on Tissues	Central Effect	Peripheral Effect
Sympathetic Calcium (group)	Reduction of surface tension	Systolic Heart musculature is stimulated	Vasoconstriction
Adrenalin	Dehydration		
Cholesterin	Striated musculature: flaccid or spastic		
H-ions	Reduction of electrical excitability Increase of oxygen consumption Increase of blood pressure		
Parasympathetic Potassium (group)	Increase of surface tension	Diastolic Heart musculature relaxed	Vasodilatation
Cholin	Hydration		
Lecithin	Muscles: increased tonicity		
OH-ions	Increase of electrical excitability Decrease of oxygen consumption Decrease of blood pressure		

In the sympathetic group effect, we recognize anxiety; in the parasympathetic group effect, sexual excitation. The parasympathetic (sexual) effect is essentially the function of *expansion* and peripheral tension, and the sympathetic (anxiety) effect is essentially the function of contraction and central tension, if we do not consider the individual organs, but rather the *overall function* of the organism. There is an antagonistic functional relationship between periphery and center. *Expansion and contraction are the basic functions which govern the total innervation of the organism.* Thus, the facts summarized in the above table reveal the following:

1. The antithesis of the potassium (parasympathetic) and the calcium (sympathetic) group: expansion and contraction
2. The antithesis of center and periphery with regard to excitation respectively
3. The functional identity of the sympathetic or parasympathetic functions with those of chemical stimulants
4. The dependence of effector innervation on the functional unity and antithesis of the total organism

Many physiological phenomena, which have not previously been understood, are explained by the functional antithesis of center and periphery. The fact that the parasympathetic system inhibits the heart but stimulates the voluntary muscles, and that the sympathetic system, on the other hand, both stimulates and contracts the heart but inhibits the muscles, does not explain the functional relationship unless we think of the musculature as part of the periphery of the individual and of the heart as being at the center. Every *fright reaction* reveals this antithesis; namely: *paralysis of the musculature of the extremities and excitation of the heart.* We see here that the functions of the organism are not bound to individual organs but are united in a lawfulness which governs the total organism, and *the organs are only the means by which these laws are implemented.* It is not the excitation of a nerve which leads to movement; instead, an impulse from the entire organism, concretely represented in its functional uniformity (plasma syncytium), is communicated to the nerve corresponding to the respective direction and function of the impulse. This fact by no means leads to teleology or to the assumption of a supra-individual entelechy. For we see now that *the functional unity of the multicellular organism is derived from the functional unity of the unicellular organism.* Both demonstrate the same two fundamental laws of expansion and contraction, not only in functional relationships but also with regard to the means and organs of execution. In both cases, there is *genetic-functional identity* of plasma and blood, plasma and nerve, plasma and muscle. It remains to be seen whether the theory of evolution will be able to confirm this functional identity. At any rate, it appears to have been proved physiologically that the same inorganic (potassium and calcium) and organic (lecithin, cholesterol) substances bring about expansion and contraction in the plasma as later these functions are carried out in the morphologically combined form of the vegetative nervous system by the sympathetic and parasympathetic. The antithesis between the two basic functions continues in the antithetical innervation of the sympathetic and parasympathetic systems. *The parasympathetic is essentially the system of peripheral excitation and central relaxation, of sexual expansion, of the direction "toward the world." The sympathetic is essentially the system of peripheral relaxation and central excitation, of anxious contraction, or, in psychological terms, the direction "away from the world—into the self."*

Now, the antithesis between sexuality and anxiety can also be classified in the overall scheme of organic natural events. Anxiety as a psychic affect is not an "expression," or a "consequence," or even an "accompanying phenomenon" of the sympathetic retreat into oneself; it is the direct inner perception of the process and is *functionally identical* to it. Likewise, sexual pleasure in the broadest and narrowest sense—namely, any sensation ranging from the simplest state of relaxed well-being to the sensual tension of excitation—is the inner perception of the parasympathetic function of expansion, which goes together with the increase in surface tension in the mechanical and electrophysiological sense. It is the inner perception of melting, merging with the world, emerging completely from oneself, and it is functionally identical with the physiological process. In this sense, and in this sense only, does the body-soul problem appear comprehensible to us. There is no longer any justification for separating in principle the "functional" nature of disease from the "organic" nature. The only differences are the routes taken by the pathogenic stimuli, and the points of attack in the biological system of the individual. At times the stimuli begin as toxic, traumatic, or physiochemical irritants; at other times they assume the form of a social inhibition of the individual's biological motility. Ultimately, they achieve the same result: *a disruption of the energy balance of the individual.** In this light, schizophrenia, for example, is not to be seen either as "psychogenic" or as "somatogenic," but rather as a disorder of vital and basic vegetative functions which is brought about in one way or another.

Though antithetical both in direction of flow and in psychic experience, sexuality and anxiety branch off from *one* stem; the specific excitations of anxiety and sexuality can

* [1945] Biopathy.

merge with each other, or even become fully separated. Thus, they are not absolute but relative antitheses; in their antithetical state they are still identical. When they begin, it is hard to distinguish sensations of anxiety in the area of the coeliac ganglion (the diaphragm and heart) from pleasurable sensations. Only what happens later decides whether the excitation develops into anxiety or pleasure.

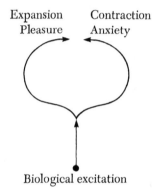

Expansion   Contraction
Pleasure   Anxiety

Biological excitation

A new view of phenomena and processes deserves careful consideration only if it permits us to reduce to a common denominator a series of facts which were previously not understood or which could be understood only by making a large number of assumptions. This principle of scientific research also has to be *proved* in the case of our hypothesis.*

* [1945] I consider it a triumph of my research method of *energetic functionalism* that the theoretical synthesis of this treatise proved to have such impressive *practical* consequences over the next ten years, as for example in the discovery of the biological energy and in cancer research.

3

The Bioelectrical* Function of Sexuality and Anxiety†

BASIC SUMMARY OF THE CLINICAL APPROACH

Up to this point, I have attempted to summarize those sexual-clinical processes which cannot be understood except in terms of a bioelectrical theory of sexuality. According to this theory, the process of sexual excitation is to be understood as an electrical charging of the erogenous zones at the surface of the organism, and the orgasm as a discharge of the potential accumulated during forepleasure.

Furthermore, on the basis of the vegetative excitation processes observed in the treatment of emotionally disturbed people, a theory evolved according to which sexuality and anxiety are seen as two excitations or "currents" of the biological organism, which stem from the same source but move in opposite directions. Sexuality would be the

---

* [1945] In reality, the processes involved are *orgonotic* and not electrical in nature. This fact could not be anticipated in 1936, when this treatise was written. Orgonotic excitation of the organism can be measured in hundreds of volts on the orgone-energy field meter. These hundreds of volts of orgonotic excitation show up on the oscillograph only as electrical millivolts. It is immediately apparent that measurements in the range of hundreds of volts and more are much more appropriate to the amount of excitation in a living organism than the millivolts of oscillographic measurements.

† First published in German, in unrevised form, by Sex-Pol Verlag, Copenhagen, 1937.

71

essence of everything that is associated with excitation, flowing, surface tension, and expansion toward the periphery. Its essential internal psychic characteristic is the sensation of pleasure. In contrast, anxiety would comprise everything having to do with current and excitation directed toward the center, away from the world. Its result would be central vegetative tension and its essential characteristic would be any sensation that can be described by the words tightness, constriction, anxiety, internal pressure, etc.

These theoretical assumptions resulted from clinical observations and sex-economic considerations. The theory endured and was fully confirmed in psychotherapeutic practice after years of testing. It was clear from the beginning that its full significance, extending beyond neurosis and character pathology, would be revealed only if it proved possible to confirm the basis of the clinical phenomena experimentally. Only after experimental testing of the theory would we know whether we had indeed hit upon an essential question of the life process, as seemed to be clearly the case, judging by clinical experience. For if sexuality and anxiety are the antithetical basic functions of living matter, then we should also be able to confirm and reproduce them experimentally.

Let me repeat the formula of orgastic excitation. The first stage of sexual excitation is increased turgor in the tissues; i.e., an increase of mechanical tension as a result of engorgement. The second stage is an increase in electrical charge at the surface (rising to climax). The third stage is the discharge of the accumulated potential through involuntary muscle contraction. The fourth stage is the mechanical relaxation following the decline of hyperemia. The "tension → charge → discharge → relaxation formula" of the orgasm required experimental testing, precisely because it seemed that fundamental life phenomena were concentrated in it. Orgasm is a basic manifestation of living substance and the tension-charge formula cannot be applied to non-living nature. After undertaking an admittedly incomplete review of the literature and making inquiries of physiologists and physicists, I concluded that there is no process in inorganic nature by which mechanical tension is converted into electrical charge, nor is there any mechanical relaxation which follows upon an electrical discharge. After the very first examination of the clinical facts, the question posed itself whether this *specifically functional connection between mechanics and electricity* constitutes the essence of biological activity. The importance of this question is obvious. The tension-charge formula, however, was only a hypothesis derived from clinical facts and concepts. If it was to lead to a useful theory and practical application, experiments would have to be carried out.

Above all else, we had to discover experimentally the nature of "vegetative current," which is so important for sex-economic clinical practice and which is at the root of sexual excitation.

Review of the literature

In the available physiological literature there is no indication of the facts revealed experimentally in connection with the tension-charge formula and the primary vegetative antithesis of sexuality and anxiety. However, test results have been reported by authors who deal with the electrical function of the skin.

The first reports about the skin as the seat of electromotive forces are found in the correspondence between C. Ludwig and Du Bois-Reymond (Akademische Verlagsgesellschaft, 1927). A distinction is made there between studies dealing with the skin as a conductor of electricity (change in resistance) and those in which the skin is treated as the generator of current and the seat of electromotive forces. H. Rein discovered that even directly adjacent areas of the skin can have quite different electrical properties. The fact that the differences in potential disappear when skin is destroyed under both electrodes was regarded by him as proof of the membrane property of skin (*Zeitschrift für Biologie*, 1926, pages 85, 195). Philip Keller discovered that the potentials of the skin are constantly changing (*Klinische Wochenschrift 2*, 1929, page 1081). C. P. Richter examined the influence of the time of year and time of day on the resistance of the skin and found that normal people have less resistance in the morning than at other hours of the day. It is clear from the various studies that no standard values can be given for the direct-current resistance of human skin, because the values vary greatly from person to person, depending on age and sex, site of the skin area tested, and the time of the day or year, etc. (Rein, *Handbuch*). Philip Keller, on the other hand, notes that there are no typical differences as regards age or sex, given ideal experimental conditions. A clear-cut negativity of the palm of the hand compared with the rest of the body was striking (56 versus 20–30 mv). Keller further notes that even gentle touching of human skin brings about a positive potential in stimulated skin zones, which is completely reversible. He postulates a relationship between skin reaction and the reaction of the sweat glands.

The above investigations into the electrical function of skin neglect to consider its erogenous function, nor do they relate skin sensitivity to this erogeneity or to the affects of sexuality and anxiety. They also ignore the differences of the specifically sexual surfaces of the organism compared with the rest of the skin. In the theoretical evaluation of the available findings, the explanation of the phenomena is sought in localized changes of the respective skin areas. Processes in the sweat glands, for example, are held responsible for generating a positive potential. Here we find that the means used by a function are confused with the function itself. In this way, the function of one skin area is delimited and cut off or isolated from the functional context of the whole organism. When, for example, the palm of the hand responds to a fright stimulus by producing a negative potential, as actually happens, and when one tries to relate this to a change in the glandular function of the palm, that is not wrong; but it conceals the fundamental fact that in a state of fright the whole organism reacts and in this case the palm is only one detail of the whole function.

In order to understand the following results, it is important to note that thus far (1) the electromotive function of the skin has been established beyond doubt; (2) the skin possesses the characteristics of a membrane; (3) the skin potentials cannot be standardized.

The theoretical summary of my experimental findings is based on the view that the electrical skin function is not localized or delimited but rather can be understood only in connection with the overall bioelectrical function of the organism; and also on the view that the skin as a membrane is only a special case, since the entire biological organism is composed of a complicated salt-electrolyte or colloid-electrolyte system, plus a membrane system. I have already described the pertinent literature, in particular the basic experimental results of Kraus, Zondek, et al., in Section 2, *Sexuality and Anxiety: The Basic Antithesis of Vegetative Life.*

Tarchanoff and Veraguth had found that skin responds to psychic stimuli with changes in potential. Tarchanoff comprehended this as a "psychogalvanic phenomenon." Not only the electrical reaction of the skin to affective stimuli, but also the nature of the functional relationship between the type of affect and the type of electrical reaction, is significant for psychopathological clinical experience. The literature dealing with the relationships between vegetative excitation and affect is so rich that we cannot give a critical detailed synopsis of it here. What is important for this present study is that in the literature about the relationships between affectivity and the vegetative apparatus there is no mention of a functional identity and simultaneous antithesis. Either the physiological phenomena are taken as "accompanying phenomena" of the affect, or the affect is considered the "consequence" of a vegetative excitation. In the first case, the affect would be taken to have no biophysiological material basis, for physiological phenomena would be merely "accompanying phenomena." In the second case, we have a mechanistic view, according to which affect would be the product of a vegetative excitation, in a similar way that so-called brain mythology considered psychic achievements to be a secretion of the brain. If we assume that affect and vegetative excitation are an inseparable and indivisible functional unit, that the one cannot be thought of without the other, several important perspectives open up for the investigations of the psychophysiological boundary area.

The present study includes genital pleasure in its experimental research. This fact needs to be strongly emphasized, because of the still prevailing timidity in scientific circles about studying sexual pleasure.

OBSERVATIONS ON THE OSCILLOGRAPH

Apart from the fundamental concept of a *primary antithesis of vegetative life,* a special hypothesis was needed at each step in the experiments; this hypothesis was based on a well-known clinical fact. In order to avoid mistakes, I had to conduct and control every experiment in such a way that it was guided by clinical theory yet was entirely unprejudiced. In the course of my work, there were many occasions when clinical theory was inadequate or took on a new aspect. Our fundamental task was to test the accuracy of the assumptions made in the tension-charge formula, or "orgasm formula," as it may also be called.

The biological resting potential

The first condition needed for the electrical function of sexuality is that the undamaged skin and mucous membrane surfaces must possess a *resting potential, or basic electrical charge.*

If one damages any area of a subject's skin by scratching the epidermis, and if one then applies an ("indifferent") electrode to this area, while the other ("differential") electrode is applied without pressure to various undamaged skin areas, then, when the subject is connected into the electrical circuit of an oscillograph, the light beam deviates from the absolute, otherwise motionless zero line. The beam jumps rapidly to a different position. This is because the electrical surface charge of the undamaged skin area has disrupted—i.e., either strengthened or weakened—the grid voltage of the apparatus, which corresponds to the absolute zero line. It is easy to prove that it is actually the undamaged skin area which causes this interference. For if one measures two abraded skin areas simultaneously, the absolute zero point does not move; the beam of light stays where it is.

Physical requirements

To help understand the experimental results,[*] we must give an idea, even if only simplified, of the physical principle behind the apparatus which produced them.

The fundamental principle is as follows: a steady electrical current is disrupted by connecting the human body into the electrical circuit. The interference is manifested as a fluctuation in the otherwise steady light beam. The light beam is generated by the reflection of light rays on a small mirror attached to the electromagnetically influenced, moving element of the oscillograph.

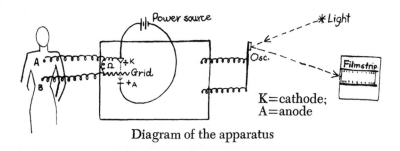

Diagram of the apparatus

It is important to understand the relationship between the electrical potential of the human body and that of the apparatus. For this purpose, it is necessary to give some information about the physical functioning of the amplifier tube to which the body is attached.

We must understand why a strong charge at the body surface generates a positive potential and a weak charge

[*] See electrophotographic data, pages 131–48.

a negative potential in the apparatus. The reason is to be sought in the function of the "amplifier tube," whose current is disrupted.

The amplifier tube consists of an evacuated glass envelope containing a glowing cathode, heated by a "filament current," and a "cold" anode. Between the two is located the grid, which is made of wire mesh. The anode is connected to the positive pole of a battery (anode battery), the cathode to the negative pole. The anode current flows as a positive current from the anode to the cathode. From the glowing cathode, electrons—i.e., negatively charged particles producing a negative current—are hurled toward the grid and the anode. The anode is positively charged and attracts the negative particles coming from the cathode, because opposite electrical charges attract one another. A voltage, the "anode voltage," exists between the anode and the cathode.

A voltage also exists between the grid and the cathode, which are connected to one another by an electrical conductor to produce a secondary circuit. The grid is negatively charged by the negative electrons that come from the cathode. Since the negative electrons impinge upon the negative grid, they are partially deflected from it, while the anode, which is positively charged, attracts the rest. The principle follows from this that the more strongly negative or the more weakly positive the charge of the grid, the more electrons it will deflect back to the cathode, the fewer electrons will get through to the anode, the weaker the resting current from the cathode to the anode will become, and the weaker also will be the grid voltage between grid and cathode. The more weakly negative or the more strongly positive the grid charge, the more electrons can get through to the anode and the stronger will be the current. In the first case, we have a "negative potential"; in the second, a "positive potential."

Now, let us connect A and B, two arbitrary spots on the human body, to the cathode and grid. If we close the circuit between the two, the light beam may stay where it is, or it may oscillate either to the left or to the right. In the first case, if it does not move, it means that the resting current of the apparatus, or the grid voltage, has not been disrupted. This can be due to two things: Both points on the body may have the same charge, so that there is no difference in charge which might show up as a voltage gradient. This is the result that is obtained if one connects two abraded places on the skin with the apparatus. If we abrade only one point, however, and leave the other untouched, then we get a voltage gradient between the undamaged and the abraded point on the skin. The voltage generated in this way interferes with the grid voltage, which we see as the absolute zero line when the body is not connected with the apparatus. The apparatus is built in such a way that this zero line does not move when the body is not connected; i.e., when the current in the apparatus, or the grid voltage, is constant. The zero line is arbitrarily determined by the design of the apparatus. Thus, a different apparatus can provide different absolute results from our own.

If the two skin areas have different charges, or if one is abraded, the light beam deviates from the zero line. If it moves to the left (with a given arrangement of the oscillograph), then the skin area directly connected to the grid has a higher charge than the grid voltage. A gradient in potential is formed from the skin area to the grid, and this charges the grid positively. As a result, as we have already said, more electrons can pass from the cathode to the anode; the current in the apparatus is increased, and a higher grid voltage is obtained. The oscillograph beam moves to the left. Conversely, the grid voltage is lowered when the skin area connected to the grid has a lower charge than the grid. In this case the electrons build up a stronger negative charge in the grid, and the current inevitably becomes weaker, since the more negative grid lets fewer electrons through to the anode.

Thus a negative-tending grid voltage indicates a decrease in the charge and a positive-tending grid voltage indicates an increase in the charge.

The choice of the direction "up" or "left" and "down" or "right" is therefore arbitrary; but it must remain the same throughout the entire experiment. If one turns on the oscillograph in reverse, or if the point to be measured on the body is connected to the cathode instead of to the grid, then some relationships reverse themselves, as is easy to see and to deduce logically. If we want to record positive charges in the top part of the curve (leftward deviation of the light beam) and negative charges in the lower part, we must attach the positive part of the body to the positive pole of the instrument in order to get deviations to the left and up.

As regards the question whether polarization of the metallic electrodes has anything to do with the phenomena, it is important to note that a resistance of approximately two million ohms between body and tube was built into our apparatus, so that practically no current flowed; only the voltage itself was indicated. Where no current flows, there is also no polarization. The current strength, which may be transmitted from the body to the apparatus, amounts to only about 10^{-6} milliampere, according to information from the manufacturer of the apparatus.

Under the conditions of the described experimental arrangement, we thus obtain the potential of the skin area to be measured in relationship to the grid voltage of the apparatus. Series of experiments have shown that once the apparatus has been set up, all the skin areas, except for the easily stimulated "ticklish" "erogenous" ones, have a *resting potential* of approximately 10 to 40 millivolts. Repeated connecting and disconnecting of the test subject always produce the same result, except for oscillations amounting to 1 to 5 millivolts. The potential of ordinary skin is the same both to the right and to the left—i.e., *symmetrical*—apart from certain exceptions, which will be discussed elsewhere.

The first electrophoto (I) shows the resting potential (RP) of a female subject (a hysteric). On the outside of the axilla to the right and left, the potential is the same; i.e., approximately −18 mv, as repeated checks confirm. As with all non-erogenous skin areas, it forms a "horizontal" line. The electrocardiographic tracing (EKG) is clearly visible and recognizable by its regularity in all the photographs. The direction of the heart spikes depends on whether one uses the right (↟) or the left (↡) arm as the site of the indifferent electrode. The reason is still unclear. The zero line of the apparatus does not change.

Horizontal regularity of the potential curve is characteristic of the biological resting potential of the undamaged surface of the organism. It indicates that *the surface carries a uniform electric charge, originating from within the organism, which rarely fluctuates in the resting state.*

The resting potential of the sexually excitable zones

Certain areas of the skin surface stand out from those which have no particular erogeneity. I am referring to those areas which are especially sensitive and responsive to stimuli during sexual activity; i.e., the penis, vaginal mucosa, tongue, lips, anal mucosa, nipples, palms, earlobes, and, strangely enough, in some intellectually oriented subjects, the forehead. *The electrical function of the sexual zones is different from that of the rest of the skin.* They have the special characteristic of exhibiting either a much higher or a much lower resting potential than ordinary skin. On the latter I have not so far been able to determine potentials of more than 0 and less than about −40 mv. However, in numerous studies of the sexual areas, I observed oscillo-graph deflections of up to +200 mv; i.e., a fifth of a volt. There are various indications that the upper limit of the chargeability of the sexual zones is difficult to determine.

At this point we encounter something that will become the crux of the overall problem: From clinical experience with emotionally disturbed patients, we know that the skin areas of sexual zones possess an intensity of sensation and excitability which far surpasses that of the rest of the skin. If these functions are intact, people experience them subjec-tively as a sensation of current, itching, flowing, pleasant feeling of warmth, etc. The non-erogenous skin areas pos-sess these characteristics either to a much lesser degree or not at all. *Can we then say that the excitation intensity of a sexual zone corresponds to its electrical charge?* To answer this question, we must point out a number of other facts.

The erogenous zones may (1) be charged electrically within the range of fluctuation of ordinary skin; or (2) their charge may greatly surpass the *upper* limit of the general surface charge.

A second fundamental phenomenon on the oscillograph explains one aspect of this peculiarity: *the light beam wan-ders; i.e., there is a gradual, continuous increase or decrease in potential.*

"Wandering" of the potential

The next electrophotograph (II) shows the electrical charge of a semi-erect penis during the course of half an hour. The apparatus is calibrated in such a way that a vertical difference in height of 1 cm corresponds to a difference of 10 millivolts. In the first measurement we see a value of approximately +35 mv, and in the second about twice that much, in relation to the grid voltage or to the damaged skin area. Checking of the zero line reveals only a minimal shift of about 3–4 mv, which can be ignored. The third measurement again is around +40 mv, and the control measurement on the nipple is approximately +20 mv; the last measurement on the penis is about +70 mv. The EKG tracing is clear. The zero line is stable at the end.

The areas marked with two crosses indicate a downward deviation toward the minus zone, and they are the result of a control carried out by *pressing* the electrode onto the penis. I will return to this later.

We must now consider certain basic facts which are essential for understanding the overall function:

1. *Potential does not increase unless an erotic flowing sensation accompanies the engorgement of the organ. The penis can thus become erect without an increase in potential taking place. The increase in potential is always linked with a psychically pleasurable sensation, and vice versa,* as will be seen later in further studies. The original assumption that erection per se is linked with a higher charge proved to be false. But this very result confirmed a mechanoelectrical hypothesis. For, *apparently, in addition to mechanical engorgement, there must be a higher surface charge in order to produce the feeling of sexual tension, which is experienced as pleasurable.*

2. The change in the level of potential does not usually

happen suddenly, but gradually. Figuratively speaking, the potential "wanders" at a faster or slower speed up or down. Repeated control tests on inorganic material revealed that this slow organic wandering has a specific character, which is easy to recognize after some practice. It is marked by a particular constancy. Inner-psychic observation of the change in the excitational sensation of current, which is linked to this constancy, reveals a striking degree of parallelism between the *quantity* of excitation and the *intensity* of sensation. (More will be said about the control experiments on inorganic matter later.)

Electrophotograph III shows a weak wandering on the left palm of a female hysteric. The potential increases, with the electrode at rest, from about +15 to +30 mv. The EKG is included in the curve. This section represents only one half of the total film record; 2.3 mm of film corresponds to about one second of elapsed time. Thus, the wandering corresponds to a change in potential over a period of about 25 seconds. (In the beginning, no attempt was made to achieve exact standardization of the results.)

In the next electrophotograph (IV), we see a wandering of the potential recorded on the same palm a few days later. When the apparatus is switched on, the potential starts at about +35 mv. It increases much more steeply; i.e., there is a much greater increase in excitation per unit time than on the first photograph. This corresponded fully to the psychic state. On the day of the second photograph, the patient was significantly more cheerful than on the first occasion.

3. *The increase in potential must be seen as the organ's response to the stimulus of gentle touching with the electrode. The amount of excitation does not correspond to the intensity of the stimulus but to the organ's state of excitation, or its readiness to be excited.*

The next two photographs, taken on different days, show the reaction of the anal mucous membrane in a female subject when touched with the KCl electrode. In photo V we see the wandering of the potential starting from about +25 mv. The subject was very happy and cheerful, and showed great interest in the level of the charge in the organ. Photo VI shows a slight fall in potential, which at first amounts to −15 mv and remains "horizontal."* On this day, the subject was suffering from premenstrual depression. *The nature and level of the potential thus indicate the psychic mood.* What is the relationship between these factors?

4. *The wandering corresponds to a preorgastic, flowing excitation or charge,* which varies in one and the same person with changes in mood.

5. *Preorgastic potential (POP) in the same erogenous area varies from person to person.* Resting potential in the non-erogenous zones, however, is approximately the same. Preorgastic potential rises from the resting potential like a mountain slope from a plain. It indicates heightened biological activity at the periphery of the organism.

In order to test the relationship between the *intensity* of the psychic sensations and the *quantity* of the electrical charge, we had to develop the experimental procedures and control experiments further.

Tickling and pressure phenomena

Until now, we have discussed only those phenomena which, without the application of external stimuli, come about from time to time at various places on the skin, thus

---

* This refutes the possible objection that the wandering might be the result of phenomena at the electrode. Electrode phenomena would have to appear *each time.* (See also "Results of the control experiments," page 113.)

indicating the peripheral electrical charge of the organism. The existence of an electrical charge of the type and configuration described is the primary precondition for the electrical function of sexuality. But this is not the entire explanation of this function.

Muscular motor activity in general and rhythmic friction, the rubbing together of pleasurably excitable body surfaces, are the fundamental biological phenomena of sexuality. From direct experience we know that they are accompanied by a sensation of sensual pleasure. But until now we have not known what constitutes the objective nature of this sensation which accompanies friction. If the electrical theory of sexuality is confirmed, then it ought to be possible to demonstrate beyond doubt that both phenomena depend on electrical changes at the site of the voluptuous sensations.

The simplest form in which sexual pleasure or voluptuousness is experienced is the sensation of *itching* or *tickling*. It automatically triggers the impulse to scratch or rub, both of which actions are related to sexual friction. At the very least, these phenomena hold true for the animal kingdom of metazoa in general.

From psychotherapeutic practice we know that a pleasurable sensation cannot be "commanded"; the more one tries to force it, the less likely it is to come about. Thus, in order to observe the phenomenon at all, it was essential to begin by creating suitable experimental conditions. The next electrogram (photo VII) shows the excitation of the tongue of a male subject, first with the electrode immobile, then being gently rubbed by the electrode, and finally with pressure being exerted three times.

In this case the experimental conditions were as follows: the indifferent electrode was applied to the left lower leg; the differential electrode, which is connected to the grid of the apparatus, was applied to the tongue without pressure. We see that when the circuit is closed, a fundamental potential of approximately +20 mv is immediately established, and it increases in the course of about 12 seconds by another 10–12 mv. The fundamental potential increases slowly, while simultaneously gentle rubbing is carried out with the electrode. Now oscillations of the potential occur around the base line; these are sometimes regular, or they sometimes deviate more into the positive or into the negative range.*

We discovered the "tickling phenomenon" all over the surface of the organism. As repeated control experiments showed, there is no such phenomenon when the electrode is rubbed on inorganic matter (cf. below). We will return to the nature of the tickling phenomenon later. For the time being, we need only remember that the arm of the curve

---

* The results presented here fit in well with phenomena already known to experimental physics. When two different substances come into contact with each other, "electrical fields" develop between the surfaces in contact or within the boundary layer. Two different bodies—e.g., a hand and hair—are each connected by a wire to an ammeter. When hand and hair gently make contact, both bodies are the molecular distance of 10^{-8} cm apart. According to the physical interpretation, the one body (e.g., the hand) gives up electrons to the other body (the hair), and the latter accumulates ("adsorbs") them somehow on its surface. In this way, an electrical field with very short lines of force is created in the boundary layer. The field is called a "double layer," and its voltage is known as the "contact voltage," the magnitude of which is in the neighborhood of approximately 0.001 to 1 volt, as in our own results. If the hand strokes over the hair, the lines of force are drawn out. The voltage between hand and hair increases to high values, and the condenser formed by the two is discharged through the ammeter. The latter indicates a surge of current by a sudden deflection of the needle. As the physical experiment shows, this experiment can be conducted on any type of body. Both can be insulators, or one of them can also be a metal. But the bodies should not both be conductors (according to R. W. Pohl, "Elektrizitätslehre," 1935, p. 196). But these physical findings and interpretations tell us nothing about the *origin* of the increased charge of an erogenous surface.

rising into the positive region is usually steep, while the arm descending into the negative region is usually more gently sloping and somewhat shorter than the rising ones. This will be important later. The EKG follows exactly all deviations in potential.

At D (= pressure), the electrode is pressed firmly, but without too much effort, into the tongue tissue. The potential falls immediately and quite steeply, by about 15–20 mv, and then rises again slowly to the previous level as soon as the pressure is released. Further, it is shown that when the potential returns, it continues its original wandering immediately, despite the interruption. The same result is obtained when the pressure is repeated three times. The pressure phenomenon is also evident in non-sexual zones, but here there is no wandering.

The next electrophotograph (VIII) shows the tickling phenomenon on the inside surface of the lower lip of a girl (KCl electrode). A negative potential formed during tickling, because the electrode pressure was unintentionally too strong. The sudden increase at K indicates the onset of strong itching. After the tickling stimulus stops, the potential falls somewhat and gradually continues wandering into the positive region.

The magnitude (size of increase) of the tickling phenomenon depends on: (1) the intensity of the pressure, in an *inverse* sense: the gentler the pressure, the steeper the increase; (2) the excitability of the stimulated area (direct relationship); (3) the psychic readiness (direct relationship).

We cannot speak of a *proportional* relationship, as long as the intensity of the sensation cannot be standardized. But everything indicates that we will find the standard we are seeking in the degree of fluctuation of potential. According to present knowledge, the fluctuation of the poten-

tial around the basic potential is itself independent both
of the excitability of the organ and also of the psychic dis-
position, and can therefore be obtained anywhere. We have
not as yet been able to detect a sharp increase in the basic
potential that is not accompanied by a simultaneous itching
sensation. The next electrophotograph (IX) shows how
large this sudden increase in the potential can be, given
appropriate psychic excitability. The charge of the palm
of the hand yields a resting potential of about +20 mv.
When the tickling stimulus is first applied, the charge suddenly jumps to about +55 mv, then falls around 10 mv,
probably as a consequence of excessive pressure, then increases again to +70 mv when the second tickling stimulus
is applied. It can be clearly seen that the EKG spikes as
well as the friction oscillations are superimposed on the
rapid increase in the basic potential. Thus, we must distinguish clearly between: (1) *the increase in the basic
potential* and (2) *the friction oscillation around the basic
potential.*

The next electrophotograph shows the electrical state of
the same palm after a pause of about one minute (X). The
basic potential does not begin at +20 mv, as previously,
but at +60 mv; it wanders slightly, then jumps to +85 mv
when the tickling stimulus is applied; during the tickling
it wanders, with clear friction phenomena, to +95 mv; when
the tickling stops, it falls slowly to about 5 mv in the course
of about 12 seconds. Applying pressure three times with the
electrode produces a decrease in potential, a drop of about
25 mv. The line resulting when one joins the points at which
the basic potential is restored after pressure has stopped
shows the direct continuation of the gradual fall in the basic
potential.

Following the observations and control experiments which
have been carried out, we can state that such regularity

in the electrical charge process cannot be obtained with inorganic matter, and that it is therefore unique to organic matter. We will return later to the general significance of this fact in connection with other experiments.

The results can be summarized as follows:

1. *Tickling stimuli, which trigger pleasurable or itching sensations, increase the electrical charge of the surface.*
2. *Pressure stimuli regularly decrease the surface charge.*

Does this conformity with a certain set of rules have a more general significance?

On another day, the same patient, in a neutral mood, produced approximately the same charge symmetrically on both the right and the left palm. In both cases, and in a control test, the basic potential remained almost steady. There was minimal wandering (photo XI).

Taking the many control experiments into consideration, we can conclude that *the excitation state—i.e., the condition of electrical charge—of a sexual organ is different at different times.*

Tickling near the electrode

When explaining the tickling phenomena, it was inevitable that the objection would be raised that they may be due to the difference in potential between the rubbing material and the skin. For that reason, the tickling phenomenon was elicited in such a way that the electrode was allowed to rest on the respective skin area while the skin adjacent to the electrode was stroked gently with dry (nonconducting) cotton wool or a feather. The tickling phenomenon appeared in the same way as if one had stroked the skin with the electrode itself (photo XII).

To determine the functional identity of the objective fluctuation in potential and the subjective sensations of tickling, the following experiment was conducted:

A control person observes the apparatus, while the subject, in a neighboring room, is connected to it with long wires. The subject, who must be skilled in self-observation, announces whether the light beam is steady, moving, or indicating a rise or fall in potential, etc. The subject does not announce this on the basis of the sensation of touch, but on the basis of the tickling sensation. The more correctly the subject is able to observe himself and the more gentle the tickling—i.e., the less contact that is made between the tickling instrument and skin—the more precise is the result. It indicates to us that the objectively visible change in potential quantitatively reflects the intensity of the pleasure sensation with "photographic fidelity." The greater the intensity of the streaming pleasure sensation, the more precisely it is reflected.

This experiment can also be carried out in reverse, with the control person announcing the reading on the apparatus and the subject checking it by assessing his pleasure sensations. Of course, this second method is not as precise and correct as the first.

The next electrophotograph (XIII) shows the result of such an experiment. We see the potential of a woman's nipple, over the period of about a minute. The differential electrode rested on the nipple and the subject tickled the areola with a dry cotton swab. The asterisk indicates when the tickling began. Until then we see a horizontal—i.e., resting—potential of about +20 mv. At the first tickling it almost shoots up, continues to increase slowly, and then increases rapidly once again before the end to about +45 mv; then it falls again as the tickling has stopped. The subject announced that she had twice felt a strong sensation of pleasure, "immediately at the start and approximately at the end." From the experiment room it was announced that the two strong readings had been recorded (this was noted down immediately). When the second increase in pleasurable sensation occurred, she had even imagined that a child was suckling her. She knew nothing of what had been going on in the meanwhile on the apparatus and said in astonishment when she saw the photograph, "That's absolutely amazing."

Since the quantity of the objective potential corresponds to the intensity of the pleasurable sensation, we can draw the conclusion that the vegetative currents of pleasurable sensation can be photographed in the form of fluctuations in the electrical charge of the erogenous surface. I will give more details later.

(The width of the beam is due to an interference from the light circuit in the building, which had not been turned off during this experiment.)

In this experimental setup it must be remembered that the control and reporting of sensations divert a person's attention, thus inhibiting the development of vegetative current. We must assume, therefore, that the quantities (or intensities) are significantly greater during spontaneous and undisturbed sexual streaming.

The same experiment was also conducted on a penis; it produced the same result. The photographic record of uniform friction next to the electrode produces an almost regular undulation. The next photograph in this experiment was taken with the apparatus set at the lowest possible sensitivity—one tenth (photo XIV).

(The deflections are in the range of about 15–20 mv.)

If friction is not accompanied by feelings of pleasure, the apparatus never shows an increase in potential. In order to conduct this experiment, it is essential that the subject be able to distinguish streaming sensations of pleasure from sensations of touch and heat.

ANXIETY AND UNPLEASURE

Current literature about the "psychogalvanic phenomenon" does not indicate whether there are any differences between pleasure and anxiety, or unpleasure. The physiologists whom I consulted felt that there was no difference; a decrease in potential would always occur. My view of the antithesis of pleasure and anxiety, which was formed on the basis of clinical observations, led me to doubt this. If psychic excitation is functionally identical to fluctuations in vegetative excitation, and the latter can be understood as fluctuations in electrical potential, then the physiologists' view cannot be correct. For pleasure and anxiety are such opposite sensations (although identical in their inception) that we can reasonably expect that their electrical directions will also be opposed. The difficulty was that, up until now, as far as I know, no distinction was made in the physiology of the skin and nerves between the directions of electrical excitation with regard to organ excitation. This distinction had to be worked out in the course of the experiments.

So far, we have had to distinguish between the absolute magnitude of a potential in its relationship to the grid voltage of the apparatus, which is arbitrarily taken as the zero line. We also determined the relative magnitude of the potential of one area of skin in comparison to another. The magnitude is relative, because both potentials are variable. We now have to determine more precisely than before a third factor; namely, the directions of fluctuation in potential.

Up to this point, we have called a potential positive if it lies above the absolute, unchangeable zero line; i.e., the grid voltage. We called it negative if it was below this zero line (e.g., +15 mv, −40 mv). We also distinguished between directions in the fluctuation of potential by speaking of the "rising" and "falling" of the potential, which can be read directly from the milliammeter of the apparatus.

We must now note the fact that any rise in potential represents a trend toward positive values, whether or not it occurs above or below the absolute zero line. Likewise, any fall in potential is a negative trend, independent of the arbitrarily determined zero line. It is no longer the absolute or relative magnitudes of the fluctuations in potential, but simply the *direction* in which they move, that is important. Thus, for example, a wandering from −40 to −20 mv is just as much a positive trend as one from +5 to +30 or from −10 to +10 mv. And, conversely, any potential is negative-trending when it wanders on the milliammeter from a higher reading to a lower one, or on the paper strip from left to right, or on the photograph from top to bottom.

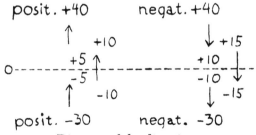

Diagram of the directions

Lowering of surface potential in anxiety and unpleasure

Stimuli which are linked with the flowing sensation of pleasure increase the electric charge of the body surface. This is expressed in the *increase in potential* or the *positive charging of the grid*. The light beam wanders to the left, the milliammeter gives higher readings, on the electrophotograph the line climbs.

The next electrophotograph (XV) shows us the curve of the movement in potential during annoyance. The experimental organ in this case was the entrance to the vagina of a woman with hysterical character traits (the same woman whose anal potential was measured). The following measurement was made on the same day on which the premenstrual anal potential (cf. VI) was measured.

The basic potential begins at about −15 mv and falls rapidly to about −25 mv. We should not forget that the patient's mood was depressed and she protested and grumbled about the procedure. She was alone in the neighboring room and was connected to the apparatus with long wires. The indifferent electrode was attached to the lower part of the leg. Both the differential and indifferent electrodes were KCl electrodes. The subject had been asked simply to apply the electrode to the labia majora. We observed the gradual drop in potential, which suddenly turned into a steep and rapid decrease. At the same moment we heard loud shouts of annoyance from the next room; a drop of KCl had fallen and irritated the sensitive mucous membrane. A cross marks this point on the photograph.

The second cross indicates the point where the subject again expressed strong annoyance; the potential fell rapidly by about 20 mv.

Annoyance, then, is accompanied by a decrease in elec-

trical charge in the sexually sensitive zones. It is now clear that sexual excitability decreases so markedly when a person is annoyed because the electrical excitation of the body moves in the *opposite* direction to that of sexual excitation; i.e., *the periphery becomes discharged instead of charged.*

The next photograph (XVI) shows us the same experiment carried out on a male subject's tongue. The basic potential starts from a resting value of about +2 mv. At point K the intentional tickling with the electrode begins; the basic potential increases gradually. At E the subject was frightened by being suddenly shouted at; the potential falls by about 20 mv. When the subject was frightened a second time, the potential dropped once more, but much less than the first time (the process was no longer photographed). On the third occasion there was no reaction at all. We see that the tickling phenomenon follows the falling basic potential without change, as does the EKG. The subject, a psychology student, drew for us the curve of the sensations on his tongue before he saw the actually recorded curve. There was an astonishing similarity between his drawing and the fundamental curve of the potential; only the tickling phenomena were lacking.

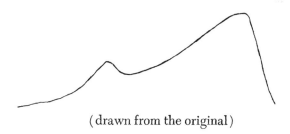

(drawn from the original)

From sex-economic clinical experience we are familiar with a remarkable phenomenon. Patients sometimes report that they experience something akin to an electrical shock on the tongue when they are frightened. *Thus, in a state of anxiety or fright, the electrical charge of the surface is decreased.* This is more marked in the sexual zones than on ordinary skin. A shrinking penis, which is a typical sign of annoyance or anxiety, also regularly exhibits a low potential.

It is easier to elicit anxiety reactions than pleasure reactions. I generally burst an air-filled paper bag or, without warning, I strike loud and hard on a gong. On one occasion, the electrical reaction did not occur. The subject informed me that at the moment when the stimulus was applied, she had become *enraged.* This raised the problem of how rage is related to the electrically negative-trending reactions of annoyance and anxiety.

Experiments have thus confirmed the sex-economic concept of the biological *primary antithesis of pleasure and anxiety;* they are opposite directions of electrical flow. *In pleasure, the surface becomes charged positively in relation to the center of the organism, and in unpleasure, annoyance, or anxiety, it becomes charged negatively.*

After the functional identity of pleasure with peripherally directed flow of current and that of anxiety with centrally directed flow had been established, the serious objection was raised that there is such a phenomenon as the so-called "cold erection"; i.e., the pleasureless erection of the penis. Experiment actually revealed that mechanical engorgement alone is not enough to produce a sensation of pleasure; if one prevents blood from draining from the male sex organ by compressing the root of the penis, the potential does *not* change. Thus, in addition to blood flow, another factor must determine excitation. The essential component of the assumed "flow" during pleasurable excitation is thus the *mechanical engorgement plus an electrical surface charge*, for a flowing sensation of pleasure occurs only when there is an increase in electrical potential, and vice versa. From this we further concluded that, *in concrete functional terms, the biopsychic direction "toward the world" and the opposite direction "away from the world, into oneself" are antithetical directions of flow of the body's bioelectrical charge*. It is as if the living organism were stretching out toward the world in the form of the bioelectrical surface charge; or as if the charging of the periphery that is associated with the pleasure process had taken over the "stretching out" function of the pseudopodium in a unicellular organism, or of a snail's feelers. And conversely, it is as if the discharging of the periphery—i.e., the lowering of its potential—were the direct expression of the "retreat into oneself." That is reason enough to examine the problem in animal experiments. But we need additional experimental proof.

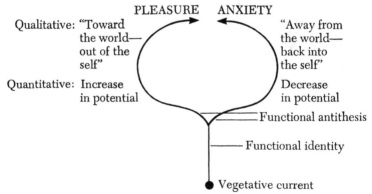

Diagram of the functional identity and antithesis
of pleasure and anxiety

MORE EVIDENCE OF THE BASIC ANTITHESIS
OF VEGETATIVE LIFE

The sugar-salt experiment

Although flowing sensations of pleasure can be produced in the tickling experiment, these sensations are not distinct nor do they indicate the scale of possible flow intensity. In our experiment, the surface of the organism is not charged artificially from the outside, but rather biologically from within; that is, from the "vegetative center." For this to occur, the test subject must be free of inhibitions, and there must be no external disturbance. All previous experiments suffered because the pleasure sensation was artificially provoked, so that it did not flow spontaneously. The result was that excitation behaved like a cautious snail, not daring to venture outside its shell. To obtain a *spontaneous* reaction, the following experiment was conducted with several people.

The cathode electrode was laid in a container with a 0.9 (normal) NaCl solution. The grid electrode was wrapped in a wad of cotton wool soaked in NaCl solution. One end of the long wad was laid on a dish containing concentrated sugar solution. The other end was also soaked in a solution of sugar or salt. The subject sucked on this end of the cotton wool while he or she put one finger into the container with the cathode electrode, in order to complete the circuit. The technical and physical correctness of this procedure will be discussed later.

A female subject, who was known to be oral-erotic, was first given *sugar* without her knowledge. As can be seen in the next electrophotograph (XVII) there is no curve in the first section, because the light beam was deflected too far to the left; i.e., so far in the positive direction that it is off

the scale. When the circuit was completed a second time, the subject had apparently to some extent grown accustomed to the stimulus. In the third section of the graph, we find an increasingly positive curve, which clearly represents the sucking movement. The pattern is similar to that produced by friction: a sharp rise followed by a more gentle fall in the curve and an increase in the ground potential. To be on the safe side, the zero line was offset to the right, into the negative range, when the circuit was closed a second time. The curve starts from at least +70 mv and increases by approximately another 20 mv. With a second subject (male), who was not so obviously oral-erotic, we observed an initial potential of about +10 mv and a further increase of about 30 mv.

When the same experiment was repeated using a *concentrated salt solution*, exactly the opposite phenomenon, with a different-shaped curve, was obtained, as follows (XVIII):

The ground potential begins at about −55 mv, and this time does not fluctuate up and down as in the sugar experiment, but falls almost in a straight line.

If one applies salt to the mouth quite without warning, then a deflection into the negative range, beyond the right-hand edge of the paper strip, is obtained, and it is as large as the deflection obtained in the opposite direction when sugar is applied.

The biological energy of the mouth quickly reaches out toward the pleasurable stimulus and retreats from the unpleasant stimulus. The antithesis of pleasure and unpleasure can thus be experimentally tested and photographed. It exists objectively, independent of our ideas of it. *The basic antithesis of vegetative life is manifested as pleasure—electrical flow directed toward the periphery—and as anxiety or unpleasure—electrical flow directed toward the center.*

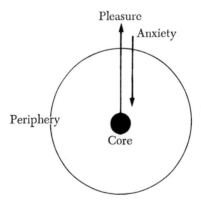

Diagram of the primary antithesis of vegetative life

The form of excitation

Up to this point, we have considered only the magnitude and direction of the excitation curve. But when we compare the sugar and salt reactions, we notice a third factor. The excitation curve in the case of the sugar reaction is very "lively." On the next photograph (XIX) we can see clearly that the potential not only increases in the positive direction (i.e., forward toward the world); it also swings far into the negative range before swinging back again strongly to the positive side. The result is deep "valleys" and steep "peaks" in the curve. If the subject sucks honey, we obtain a similar pattern with only slight changes: each increase in excitation is preceded by a decrease. This phenomenon is, however, absent in the salt reaction. Here (photo XX) we find only a less uniform "quiet" retreat, after the basic potential has dropped steeply; i.e., "retreated." In other subjects, even the minor fluctuations in excitation (here about 2 to 3 mv) are lacking; the excitation falls steadily.

Disappointment reaction

If one administers first sugar and then salt, the reaction occurs in the manner described, though in varying degrees. We also observed the effect of *habituation;* namely, that repeated doses administered in the same sequence reduce the sugar reaction. The increase in potential becomes less each time, and the salt reaction no longer elicits as intense a swing in a negative direction as the first time, when the stimulus was unexpected. However, if one first administers salt and then sugar, the full negative salt reaction will be obtained, but the positive sugar reaction does not occur; the sugar, too, will elicit a strong negative reaction.

This finding speaks clearly for the *biological* nature of these reactions. After salt has been administered, the tongue behaves as if it has become cautious, and will no longer allow itself to be enticed. It now reacts with anxiety to sugar as well. Repeated experiments showed that when sugar is administered, an increase in the electrical charge of the tongue is not obtained until about half an hour to a whole hour later. Even then, the rapid surge of charge, such as occurred when sugar was first administered, was lacking, as were the lively reactions of the kind illustrated in photo XIX. The friction potentials, which were supposed to correspond to sucking, fluctuated only very slightly and "sluggishly," as it were.

Aside from direction and intensity, we can distinguish various degrees of *liveliness* in the character of motor activity in all bioelectrical excitation phenomena. In the same organ, the same stimulus can produce lively and rapid responses in one affect state, and in another affect state slow and indistinct responses, as if the organ were "sluggish." From these facts we can draw the following conclusions:

1. The biophysical reaction of sexual organs does not correspond to the stimulus, but instead depends on the state of readiness of the organism.
2. A "disappointed" organ reacts sluggishly and "cautiously."
3. When an organ is "accustomed" to the stimulus, the positive or negative potential decreases; the positive and negative reactions are closer to the zero line.

These experiments confirm some well-known aspects of erotic relationships.

The reaction to a sexual partner is not always, or only occasionally, directly correlated with the attractiveness of that person. It is essentially dependent on the state of sexual readiness.

We know that disappointment reactions of the genitals occur in sexual activity. When serious genital anxiety or unpleasure has been or is being experienced, genital excitation is difficult to achieve, or it happens sluggishly, if at all. Instead of erection or vaginal secretion, the respective organs shrink or dry up, or vaginismus occurs. The organ is governed by the urge to withdraw; therefore, the opposite reaction—erection, "striving toward the world"—is impossible to achieve. Thus, in cases of impotence and frigidity, it is not so much a matter of whether a genital threat was actually experienced, but whether the genital organ responded with a biologically negative anxiety reaction, and this has become fixed. The psychic experience of genital anxiety is effective only when it becomes structured in the negative biophysical reaction. I will return later to the topic of *pleasure anxiety*.*

PREREQUISITES FOR THE PLEASURE REACTION

The findings reported here can be verified only if one familiarizes oneself with the special characteristics of peripheral bioelectrical charge inhibition, which we have referred to as "caution." The charge "does not dare to come forward" when third parties are present, when a disruption is possible, or when attention cannot be diverted completely from the outside world. For this reason, a series of complicated measures was necessary to obtain incontestable results.

It is not so much the increase in charge as the magnitude of the fluctuations in potential which seems to be crucial for the full biophysical excitation of the periphery. We see in the sugar reactions that the peaks in the charge are

---

* [1945] The biophysical disappointment reaction leads to resignation, shrinking of the organs, and even to a loss of substance, as in the case of the carcinomatous shrinking biopathy. Cf. "The Carcinomatous Shrinking Biopathy" and "Results of Experimental Orgone Therapy in Humans with Cancer" [chapters V and VIII in *The Cancer Biopathy*.—Ed.].

separated by deep "valleys," which correspond to strong withdrawal of charge. From clinical experience we know that the voluptuousness of a sex act is all the more intense the greater the waves of excitation that are produced with each friction. If excitation increases steadily, the act is not experienced with such intense pleasure, even if in the end the same level of potential is reached. Thus, the important thing seems to be the *alternation of rest and activity*, the replacement of a deep discharge by the maximum possible renewed charge.

The curve representing any tickling phenomenon consists of two parts, one directed upward and one pointed downward. The former corresponds to a buildup of charge, the latter to a decrease in charge. We cannot arbitrarily call this a discharge. If we use an analogy taken from the motor behavior of animals that suckle, we can understand this a little better. We can compare the electrical charge of the sugar-licking tongue with a suckling calf, which retreats from the mother's teat only to thrust forward again even more energetically. What we see here is probably a continual renewal of motor activity, an advance to new pleasure. One thinks instinctively of a tiger crouching before the leap: contraction before maximum stretching (expansion). Since the contraction in this case does not express relaxation, but instead extreme inner tension, and since also the peripheral charge corresponds to a tension which is directly perceived, two different kinds of tension must be involved. At the beginning of the leap, the tension is *centrally* located in the organism; *peripheral* motor activity of the organism increases in direct proportion to the intensity of the central tension. The withdrawal of charge from the periphery must necessarily lead to an increase in the central tension. *The excitation shoots from the center to the periphery.* This central tension can be perceived directly if, for example, during coitus, one interrupts particularly pleasurable friction and remains still. Then an impulse from the center sparks renewed friction, which builds up peripheral charge. We will be able to observe this back and forth of excitation in detail further below.

Accordingly, we must distinguish carefully between four types of negative electrical reaction at the periphery:

1. Central tension resulting from peripheral charge
2. Peripheral orgastic discharge
3. Anxiety reaction
4. Extinction of the source of tension—death, following biopathic shrinking

In all four types, the surface potential falls. In the first, a recharge occurs, and the result is *pleasure*. In the second, the charge drops below the resting potential and returns to the zero state; this is the process of *orgastic discharge*. In the third, the tension remains central: *anxiety*. The fourth type of negative electrical reaction corresponds to *death*. According to present experimental findings, dying tissue takes on a negative charge; the central source of charge is extinguished and the organism gradually shrivels.

If we distinguish between the different functions of the same negative direction of biophysical excitation, we will be better able to bring some order into the wealth of phenomena.

ELECTRICAL EXCITATION IN KISSING

Inadequacies of direct measurement

From the start of our experimental work, our goal was to accomplish the main experiment; i.e., to record on film the electrical excitation occurring during the sexual act. But the experimental arrangement in the first experiments, in which we attached the electrode *directly* to the place on the surface where the measurement was to be carried out, made it improbable that the intended goal could ever be attained. Direct measurement of the electrical charge of the genitals during coitus is impossible. The manipulation alone would suppress any excitation. Also, direct measurement is not totally free from mechanically induced fluctuations in the values obtained; e.g., disruptions may be caused by a broken contact. Finally, there was one other concern which had to be eliminated. Although the control experiments showed that rubbing the electrode or its rubber-covered end against glass or an electrolyte-moistened cloth produced no fluctuations, it was nevertheless necessary to ensure that the results were not affected by mechanical processes at the electrode. At first there was no answer, because I could see no other way but measuring excitation directly. At this state of the investigations, we obtained the next photograph of excitation during ejaculation (XXI).

The subject's orgasm was disturbed (masturbation had to be stopped just before ejaculation). During ejaculation, the electrode (KCl) rested on the glans penis. At the start of the climax, a positive trend in the basic potential occurs; then, at regular intervals corresponding to uniform periods of time, the potential rises in steep peaks of about 10 mv each. We cannot say with certainty whether the second large positive trend with its two separate peaks represents, like the first three-peaked excursion, bursts of ejaculation. Since 2.3 mm on the photograph corresponds to a time of one second, as can be clearly seen on the EKG, probably only the first three-peaked positive movement corresponds to the ejaculation, while the other peaks correspond to the post-ejaculatory contractions of the penis. The regular spacing and also the more or less regular (although slightly decreasing) height is indicative of the biological character of the phenomena. The basic potential also decreases after an initial rise.

There are uncertainties, both because of the technical difficulties and because of the demands of the psychic situation. But the basic characteristics of the phenomenon cannot be doubted. The form of electrical excitation, of the rise and fall in potential, corresponds to what one would expect, based on clinical experience. The drop in orgastic excitation must in principle (independent of the magnitude) be equal to the rise; it does not have the gradient of the rise. After ejaculation has taken place, the basic potential remains steady; i.e., in the horizontal plane in the photograph at −25 mv. We must point out here that the orgastic excitation curve in this instance does not exhibit the deep negative plunges of the pre-orgastic friction curve; instead, it rises above the basic potential in the positive direction only.

The technique of indirect measurement

In order to carry out the main experiment in such a way that psychic disruptions were eliminated as completely as possible, we had to find a way to measure excitation *indirectly*. For this purpose, we had to determine whether the potential of two surfaces rubbing rhythmically together could be detected when two fingertips are used as the measurement sites. The experiment could only give correct results if (1) the potential indicated corresponded in form to the excitation of the sites being tested; (2) the direct measurement sites, the fingertips, were held still; (3) the basic potential of two skin surfaces touching together remained the same, independent of the size of the contact surfaces.

In the following three electrophotographs we see:

1. The resting potential of two hand surfaces touching each other (XXII)
2. The pressure phenomenon elicited by pressing one of the fingertips against the glass bottom of a container (XXIII)
3. The rise in potential which results when two people touch their palms gently together (XXIV)

The measurement is carried out in the following way:

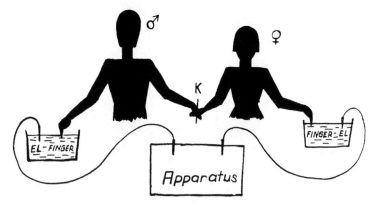

In the first photograph we see the EKGs of both subjects superimposed on the tracing. The resting potential appears at its familiar setting of about −20 mv. When at rest, the basic potential is horizontal. On the second photograph, we see some negative spikes, which correspond to vigorous rubbing of one fingertip on the glass bottom of the electrolyte container. On the third photograph, we see strong positive-trending spikes up to +20 mv, thus amounting to about 40 mv elicited by gentle stroking. Direct observation showed that any harder contact changed the positive trend into a negative trend; i.e., a *fall* in potential. After the stroking stopped, the basic potential dropped gently again to the previous resting potential.

The next photograph (XXV) impressively illustrates the *antithesis* of pleasure and pressure. It shows pressure applied in a handshake, alternating with the palms being gently rubbed together. The results were directly observed. Each rise in potential corresponds exactly to a feeling of well-being; each negative excursion corresponds to strong pressure. Overall, there is a slight increase in the basic potential. The subjects were two women.

The results of these experiments remind us of our clinical experience that gentle friction during intercourse increases pleasure and strong friction decreases it.

We will now add a report about the main control experiment. In the next photograph (XXVI), we see the respective potentials obtained when various skin surfaces were touched:

Two fingertips	about −10 mv
Two finger surfaces	about −20 mv
Two palms	about −10 mv
Two forearms (outer surfaces)	about −20 mv
Two forearms (inner surfaces)	about −20 mv

Encouraged by these incontestable results, I photographed the following kiss exchanged by a happy couple (XXVII). We see the already familiar frictional excitations; i.e., steep peaks, separated by deep valleys.

The next electrophotograph (XXVIII) shows the frictional excitation in "slow motion" and greatly magnified. One centimeter horizontally equals one second; vertically, one centimeter equals about 3.33 mv.

Overall, the basic potential increases. We see that each excitation peak is essentially similar in shape. But the details remained uninvestigated.

The next photograph (XXIX) shows us the course of excitation when a kiss exchanged by the same couple becomes unpleasurable. The woman very soon expressed strong displeasure; the basic potential declines and the fluctuations due to friction likewise grow smaller. Finally, we see an abrupt drop toward negative values, denoting annoyance. This picture was taken with the film running fast through the camera—1 cm equals 1 second—as in slow-motion photography. (As control tests on inorganic matter revealed, the fluctuations around the base line correspond to oscillations of the oscillograph itself.) From this, we conclude that the *magnitude of the potential* (except for negligible differences) *is independent of the size of the area of the two skin surfaces touching each other without moving, when they are unexcited.*

On the basis of these experiments and the controls that were carried out, we now recorded, by means of indirect measurement, a naked embracing couple, when the man was kissing the woman's breast (XXX).

The basic potential is at about +100 mv; the frictional fluctuations of the kiss are about 10 mv each, as usual. We see the two EKG's. The bodies were resting together. The total excitation was greatly impaired by the conditions of the experiment, but nevertheless it reached +100 mv. From this, we were entitled to draw conclusions about the level of full sexual excitation that can be achieved during undisturbed coitus. The question now was no longer whether there was an electrical charge and discharge during coitus, but rather whether, due to the magnitude of the charge, it could be recorded at all from a photographable zero line.

RESULTS OF THE CONTROL EXPERIMENTS

The electrical phenomena at the erogenous zones would have no far-reaching importance if they did not correspond to *specifically biological excitation processes;* that is, if they could be duplicated on inorganic matter. We have already referred to the control experiments on inorganic matter. I will now present a summary of them.

Errors due to poor insulation

If the leads or the electrodes are poorly insulated, spikes can appear on the oscillograph which do not originate from the place on the body being measured. For example, if a third person or the person in charge of the experiment touches the subject who is connected to the apparatus, the light beam is rapidly deflected from its resting position *toward negative values.* The degree of the negative deflection varies according to the individual doing the touching. This source of error is easily recognized, because the original level of the potential is soon regained. The deflections disappear if the touching is repeated frequently. We note that the effect is negative and thus is not a source of error for *positive* potential effects.

Poorly insulated electrodes produce spikes on the oscillograph, but they are always negative-trending; i.e., current-reducing. The leads to the electrodes must be firmly connected; when the machine is switched on, mechanical vibration of the wires results in oscillations which cannot be controlled. If one does not use a Faraday cage, *all light circuits must be turned off;* otherwise, disruptive oscillations are recorded on the apparatus. Potentials can still be measured, but the light beam will be blurred.

Can the phenomena we have described be due to extraneous effects occurring at the electrodes?

Non-polarizable electrodes of 0.1 N potassium chloride solution were used for the *direct* measurements. Handled correctly, the electrodes never give readings that deviate by more than a maximum of 0.5 mv from each other. The hand-held electrodes are insulated with glass and rubber and protected by metal casings. Neither rubbing the end of the electrode against the bottom of the glass container nor warming the KCl solution causes the beam to deviate. No fluctuations in the readings were caused when the leads to these KCl electrodes were touched at various places.

In the case of *indirect* measurement, silver electrodes were used. If one immerses two electrodes of pure silver in a KCl solution and closes the circuit, rapid negative deviations of varying magnitude occur. But if one wraps the ends of the silver electrodes in cotton wool saturated in KCl solution, and then lays these ends on two pieces of cotton wool saturated in KCl which hang down into the KCl container, no deviations worth mentioning are recorded.

Can the concentration of the electrolyte be a source of error?

At first, only KCl electrodes were used. Since this solution had a disruptive effect when measurements were carried out on a mucosal surface, 0.9 N NaCl solution was later used. In order to test whether the different ions and concentrations could be the source of error, the following controls were repeatedly performed:

1. Silver electrodes connected with cotton wool soaked in 0.1 KCl usually produce no fluctuation; only rarely do deviations of up to about —5 mv occur.
2. Similarly, silver electrodes connected by cotton wool soaked in a 0.9 N NaCl solution give steady readings.
3. If one concentrates the salt solution, the position of the zero line does not change.
4. If one uses a concentrated sugar solution, deviations of up to 10 mv are observed.
5. If one pours a concentrated NaCl solution over the cotton wool soaked in 0.1 N KCl, fluctuations between —5 and —10 mv are seen.

If one does not connect the silver electrodes directly, but allows a strip of cotton wool soaked in 0.9 N NaCl to hang down from each electrode and dip into different solutions, the following observations are made:

There is no deviation in the NaCl solution.
Deviations of up to about —10 mv occur in concentrated sugar solution.
Deviations of up to about —10 mv also occur in concentrated sugar solution mixed with concentrated salt solution.

The probable reason why the concentration plays such an insignificant role is that a 2 million ohms resistor is con-

nected between the tube and the electrodes, and this does
not permit current to flow, but only indicates voltage. Thus,
the phenomena in the sugar-salt experiment are not ob-
scured by the effects of concentration, even if we ignore
the unmistakable biological phenomena.

Can the tickling, pressure, and stroking phenomena which we have described be obtained in inorganic matter?

If one connects the two electrodes via a piece of cloth
soaked in KCl or NaCl, the oscillograph reading deviates
by about 20–40 mv into the negative range when the circuit
is closed. But no manipulation of the cloth with insulated
material produces any fluctuation in the reading. However,
if one rubs or presses the cloth with a finger, the typical
wanderings, etc., appear at once. Thus, if we are too critical about the findings made on organic matter, and if we
are not guided by the same critical spirit in the control
studies—if, for example, we press the silver electrodes into
the cloth with our finger—we can easily believe that "the
cloth, too, is alive" (XXXI).

If the distance between the measurement sites on the
cloth is increased, thereby raising the resistance, the result
is just as negative.

When testing new findings, it is easy to be careless, simply in order to disprove something. I owe the discovery
of a new problem, whose solution has not yet been found,
to just such a "disproving" experiment. A catatonic was
connected to the apparatus; the differential electrode was
laid on the back of his hand, and next to it he was tickled
with dry cotton wool. We observed the familiar tickling
phenomena. In order to verify the results, the cloth on
which the hand was lying was soaked in KCl and stroked
with cotton wool; the same fluctuations resulted. The situa-

tion seemed hopeless. Only on the following day did it occur to me that during the control experiment the indifferent electrode *had not been removed* from the catatonic's leg. Thus, a circuit existed: leg–body–hand–soaked cloth. True, the control experiment was invalidated, but the big question remained: why had the tickling phenomena still appeared, as if the ability of organic tissue to produce tickling phenomena *had been transferred to the soaked cloth?* At present we cannot understand this fluctuation produced on "living cloth."*

With one exception, no increase in potential can be obtained on inorganic matter under the same test conditions, but the restriction must be added that this is true *only as far as present research goes.* If one touches two connected electric plugs, there is no fluctuation in potential; if one immerses them in a solution, the potential declines considerably and at a fast rate.

One can obtain fluctuations by rubbing the electrodes on metallic material; however, the deviations are toward negative values only, they cannot be reproduced, and they are completely arhythmical.

If electrodes are rubbed on an electric flashlight, positive deviations are also obtained. But it is clear at once that they do not have the rhythm of organic wandering (XXXII). The increases are arhythmical or mechanical and angular. The surface of the flashlight is charged electrically from the inside and thus acts like a living body. But the fluctuations are different.

The control experiments we have described reveal that the excitation phenomena cannot be produced on inorganic matter.

---

* [1945] In the meantime we have come to understand this phenomenon: the orgone *field* of the hand behaves in a *biological* way on damp cloth.

On some photographs, the spikes of the EKG point upward and on others downward. The direction of the cardiac spikes is independent of the direction of the sexual excitation phenomena. The positive direction during tickling remains the same (upward) whether or not the cardiac spike points upward or downward. As special control tests reveal, a positive cardiac spike is obtained when the left fingertip is laid on the cathode and the right fingertip on the grid. The spike points downward when, conversely, any of the right fingertips is laid on the cathode and a left fingertip on the grid. At the present time there is no explanation for this phenomenon. It probably has something to do with the direction of the heart-muscle action current, which is determined by the contraction of the heart. It undoubtedly reflects the fluctuation of potential on the skin, which originates from the heart. Inner perception shows us that every heartbeat is linked with a pulse of sensation, which we localize in the cardiac region. This phenomenon is nothing other than the incipient stage of a sensation of the kind which is fully developed in pleasure or anxiety. The details are still not clear.

If we connect up with a simple radio, instead of with an oscillograph, the fluctuations in potential are converted into sound instead of light. The constant muted hum of the radio disappears completely when the two electrodes are connected by cotton wool which has been soaked in electrolyte. This corresponds to the negative deflection of the light beam. When indirect measurements are taken from palms that are touching together, rhythmical stroking produces rhythmical sound phenomena. *With gentle stroking, the intensity of the sound is increased; with pressure, it is decreased.* This corresponds fully to the fluctuations of the light beam in the oscillograph.

THE "VEGETATIVE CENTER"

Experimental investigations of skin potentials during pleasure and anxiety confirmed the assumption that there are two opposite directions of bioenergy flow during excitation: *toward the periphery* and *toward the center*. We now understand clearly the nature of the flow. During pleasure excitation or anxiety excitation, it is not the blood flow alone that determines the sensation of streaming, but rather the transportation of quanta of electrical charge by the blood and lymph flow.* We have known for a long time that ions are transported in the blood. Now the skin, as a vegetative periphery, proves to be the site of the peripheral concentration of or reduction in the quantities of electrical charge. The direction "toward the world," on which we were forced to base the sex-economic theory of drive, is clearly confirmed. Less clear until now was the nature of the direction "away from the world, into the self." Where does the bioelectrical flow go in the case of anxiety? This question concerns the localization of the *vegetative center*.

Where in the body should we look for the areas from which biological energy springs and to which it retreats? Our initially hypothetical answer is that the areas in question are the *ganglia plexuses of the vegetative nervous system, and above all the plexus coeliacus, plexus hypogastricus, and Frankental's genital plexus*. In the near future I will provide clinical proof of this assumption. *The vegetative nervous system represents the generator; i.e., the producer of bioelectrical energy in the human body.* The experimental studies presented in the first part of this work

---

* [1945] Correction: transportation of *orgone charges*.

fully support this hypothesis. Let us now test how far this assumption takes account of the clinical facts and is able to render comprehensible those phenomena of neurosis pathology and affect pathology which have hitherto eluded interpretation.

In the process, we must free ourselves from a prejudice which tends to dominate neurological and medical thought in general. The term "center" has up to now been used to mean the "cerebrum" and the most closely linked switching stations of neural excitation in the medulla oblongata. The time has not yet come to discuss in detail the justification for this term. Instinctively, the cerebrum is seen as the actual center and the *origin* of all impulses, which are then transmitted to the rest of the body. The cerebrum would thus, so to speak, control what men do. True, neuropathology in recent years (I refer especially to the work of Goldstein) has attempted to introduce an entirely new way of thinking, which seems to take away the supreme function so far attributed to the cerebrum. All branches of medicine have shifted their interest to research on the vegetative functions, in particular those of the parasympathetic and sympathetic systems. In addition, zealous attempts are being made to analyze the essential characteristics of this apparatus and its relationship to psychic life. My view of the function of the parasympathetic and sympathetic systems—i.e., of the *basic antithesis of vegetative life*—is in total harmony with this new direction and in many points it refutes the mechanical physiology of the cerebrum. It would be premature to enter into this discussion now, but it was necessary to mention this in order to make it clear that the expression "vegetative center" means not only the center of the vegetative neural apparatus but the center of all biophysiological and character-affect functions. Expressed cautiously, the cerebrum, according to this hypothesis, would be merely a specially designed apparatus for implementing and inhibiting the *general vegetative bodily functions*. The irrefutable fact that life can function biologically long before a cerebrum is developed is proof of this assumption. The affects with which we have been so concerned—namely, *pleasure, anxiety, and rage*—are in no way linked to the existence of the cerebrum. *The vegetative function is phylogenetically older than the cerebral function.* The expression "vegetative center" is thus more comprehensive than it would seem at first glance. It is necessary to assume that the functions of the cerebrum also depend on the general vegetative functions.

If a grid electrode is placed above the navel, approximately halfway between it and the lower end of the costal cartilages, the abdominal skin has the usual potential of about -20 to -40 mv. If one then presses a finger into the abdomen next to the electrode, the potential falls steadily by about 10–20 mv. The same thing happens when the patient is asked to press as when in defecating, or to inhale deeply. The objection that the fall in potential occurs as a result of pressure on the skin is disproved by the fact that the potential decreases in the same way when the subject inhales deeply. When the subject exhales, the potential increases slowly again to its original level. In patients who have a rigid diaphragm and are unable to *ex*hale fully, the fluctuation in potential when they inhale and exhale is not as clear or as extensive as that in subjects who are able to breathe freely.

This symptom is worth thorough consideration. When a person inhales, the diaphragm descends and presses on the organs located below it. The abdominal cavity contracts while the thorax expands. Conversely, when a person exhales, the thorax contracts while the abdominal cavity expands. A second phenomenon points in the same direction. If a subject inhales deeply, any vegetative streaming sensation that might exist in the epigastric region disappears. However, if the subject exhales deeply, a sensation similar to anxiety or pleasure is experienced in the epigastric region and in the lower section of the thorax.

An anatomical view of the organs in the abdominal cavity, together with the experimental results, explains the facts described. We can see how two important organs situated below the arch of the diaphragm are influenced mechanically by the displacement of the diaphragm. These organs are the stomach, and behind it the *solar plexus,* which is the largest plexus of the vegetative nervous system. From previous experiments, we have learned that pressure reduces electrical-charge activity. We had to make the further assumption that the skin is continuously supplied with a bioelectrical resting current from an "as yet unidentified center." *The charge of the skin decreases in the case of pressure and anxiety.* In pleasure, the biological energy of the body stretches toward the world; it withdraws in anxiety. Let us picture now the situation of the organs which encircle the abdominal plexus and pelvic plexus in a state of fright. (1) The breath is drawn in deeply and the shoulders are hunched; (2) the abdominal muscles are tightly tensed; and (3) the pelvic floor is raised rapidly.

In anxiety, therefore, the abdomen behaves like a living being with something to protect. The walls close more tightly around its contents. Without doubt, it is the highly sensitive system of ganglia in the abdomen and pelvis which is being protected. The only possible interpretation that can be put on the drop in potential of the skin of the abdomen when a person strains his bowels or pulls in his stomach is that pressure is being exerted on the plexus, thereby impeding its bioenergetic activity. This observation will be further corroborated in a later presentation of clinical facts.*

Contractility of the vegetative nervous system

My previous description of the vegetative function might easily have led to an error. The parasympathetic and sympathetic systems are two branches from one and the same stem but producing opposite effects. One branch is associated with the pleasure function, and the other with the anxiety function. Certain aspects of vegetative behavior tell us that this view is inadequate for understanding the total vitality of the vegetative function. It would be justifiable to object that the directions "out of the self" and "into the self" alternate during orgasm or in muscular movement. Can one then claim that only the parasympathetic system is involved in the experience of sexual pleasure, and only the sympathetic system in the case of anxiety? Surely there is such a thing as anxiety-induced diarrhea, which is influenced by the parasympathetic system! The objection is well-founded and forces us to examine much more accurately the antithetical character of the vegetative function. The schematic contrasting of parasympathetic and sympathetic system is in fact incorrect. Physiological anatomy does not claim that the parasympathetic and sympathetic systems are two totally separate anatomical systems; it merely identifies the paths of neural excitation. It is probably closer to reality to assume that

---

* [1945] In the following ten years, this physiological fact became the basis of vegetotherapy, the new technique in the treatment of biopathies. Cf. *The Function of the Orgasm.*

we are dealing here with a functionally and morphologically uniform system which can function in two opposite directions. Thus, the functions of stretching and contracting would be executed by *one and the same* organ, and this vegetative apparatus can assume three different positions: (1) *the middle position of equilibrium* between peripherally directed and centrally directed excitation; (2) *the position of extreme contraction* (state of fright, hypersympatheticotonia); (3) *the position of extreme expansion* (sexual excitation, hypervagotonia).

I have assumed instinctively that *the vegetative nervous system is contractile;* i.e., it not only conducts excitation but also behaves like a mass of plasma which expands and contracts. This assumption is *indispensable.* I would like to present some arguments which explain why it is necessary:

1. Studies with the oscillograph reveal that pleasure and anxiety are identical with the increase or decrease of the bioenergetic charge at the periphery. *The intensity of sensation reflects the quantity of charge.* From this, we can conclude that vegetative sensations directly reflect the state of vegetative excitation.

2. Physical sensations directly mirror the process of stretching and contraction. We must regard the vegetative sensations as a reflection of real bodily processes. The abdominal cavity and pelvis are the seat not only of the most intense vegetative sensations but also of the densest vegetative nerve plexuses.

3. The process of the filling and emptying of blood vessels directly parallels expansion and contraction.

4. We can see the function of the contraction and expansion of vegetative substance in molluscs, worms, snails, as well as in the plasma of amoebae. The swelling of the substance, which leads to expansion, is accompanied by a

buildup of charge; the relaxation occurring with contraction is accompanied by a decrease in charge.

5. The vegetative nervous system is a *uniform* plexus, running through all the organs of the body, right down to the smallest parts. It is a uniform network of plasma. The vegetative involuntary "innervation" can be nothing other than the process of charge and discharge itself, which occurs together with the swelling and shrinking of the tissue.

Therefore, the concept that the parasympathetic and sympathetic nervous systems are separate from and opposed to each other, with first the one (pleasure) and then the other (anxiety) functioning, can now be corrected as follows: *the vegetative nervous system has the ability to contract and expand.* From the middle position of *vegetative equilibrium,* it is able to move in the direction toward the world (i.e., to stretch), or to retreat into itself (i.e., to contract). It can also swing from one direction to the other or remain fixed in either of the extreme states. Putting it in somewhat simplified terms, the state of vegetative equilibrium is one where neither expansion positions nor contraction positions have become established. *Vagotonia* would correspond to a *fixed* state of expansion, and *sympatheticotonia* to a *fixed* state of contraction. *Muscular armor* implies a biopathic state of equilibrium whose function it is to *avoid* the anxiety of contraction as well as the pleasure of expansion and orgastic convulsion.

The vegetative nervous system is thus a contractile plasma system, a contractile organ running through the entire organism. It represents the "*amoeba in the multicellular organism.*" *This is the explanation and basis of the uniformity of the total body function.* The "animal in man," the "devil in the flesh," actually exists as the most primitive element of nature; it unites the human animal and the motile mass of plasma.

SOME THEORETICAL CONCLUSIONS

In the following, the conclusions drawn from the experimental verification of the orgasm theory will be briefly presented.

1. Sexual excitation is functionally identical to bioenergetic charge of the erogenous zones. Anxiety excitation goes together with a decrease in the surface charge. The concept of "libido" as a yardstick of "psychic energy" is no longer a mere metaphor, but applies to energetic processes. Thus, the sexual function is one of the general electrical* processes that occur in nature.

2. The skin and mucous membranes possess a resting potential (RP) which varies within certain limits in one and the same individual and corresponds to the unexcited state. The resting potential corresponds to the permanent, uniform bioelectrical charge of the surface of the organism.

3. The vegetative ganglia apparatus ("vegetative center"), together with the total biological electrolyte and membrane system, is the source of the surface charge. The erogenous zones are capable of registering extremely intense sensation and of generating high bioelectrical† charge. As surface zones, which are more easily and intensely excitable than the rest of the skin, they not only have a higher resting potential in general, but also their potential fluctuates over a wider range, in keeping with their state of excitation. A higher electrical potential also corresponds to a more intense state of excitation, which is experienced subjectively as a more intense sensation of excitation or current. Likewise, a decline in excitation is matched by a

---

* [1945] Orgonotic.
† [1945] Orgonotic.

decline in potential. Specific sensations of pleasure or unpleasure are different from the simple sensations of pressure or touch which are not associated with pleasure or unpleasure. Clinical experience has also shown that the states of sexual excitation or of anxiety differ both in the intensity and in the way in which they are experienced from all other sensations. Therefore, in experiments, too, they can be clearly distinguished from all other processes.

4. The simplest form in which erogenous excitation occurs is the sensation of itching or tickling. The potential of an erogenous zone differs, depending on whether an itching or a tickling sensation is present or not. What our patients in the end stages of character-analytic treatment describe as a new "streaming" or "sweet sensation" or "shudder of pleasure," etc., is to be understood as a state of preorgastic excitation or a preorgastic increase in potential. Depending on the gradient of the intensity of the sensation, this preorgastic excitation is matched by an equivalent gradient in the rise in electrical* potential in the zone in question.

5. The passive mechanical congestion of an erogenous organ does not bring about a rise in charge above the resting potential. In contrast, the vascular congestion or tissue turgor which follows erogenous stimulation and which is connected with pleasurable sensations produces a clearly visible increase above the resting potential. Thus, the mechanically produced engorgement must be joined by an electrical charge of the surface in order to produce an erotic sensation; i.e., in order to be "sexual." The positive results of these experiments prove the correctness of the assumption that the leap from mechanical tumescence to electrical†

* [1945] Orgonotic.
† [1945] Orgonotic.

charge is a specifically *sexual-biological* process. The first part of the orgasm formula is confirmed.

6. Sexual friction is a biological activity which is governed by the alternation of charge and discharge. Discharge is always pleasurable; charge is always pleasurable, provided it is followed by discharge.

7. From his or her subjective feelings in the course of excitation, a psychically undisturbed subject who is capable of both orgastic and preorgastic sensations is able to indicate the readings being obtained by the recording apparatus (rise, fall, etc.). *The intensity of the pleasurable sensation corresponds to the quantity of electrical surface charge, and vice versa.*

8. These experimental results are very important for the theory of the body-soul relationship. If preorgastic and orgastic potential does indeed exist, and if the corresponding *sensations* are exact reflections of the objectively verifiable *excitation* process, then *the functional identity and antithesis of the bodily processes and the pleasure-unpleasure sensation* is proved. *The quantity of surface potential and the intensity of the erogenous or vegetative sensations are functionally identical.* It remains to be explained why non-erogenous sensations, such as sensations of touch and pressure, do *not* produce a rise in potential.

9. Since only vegetative sensations of pleasure are accompanied by an increase in peripheral charge, and since unpleasure, anxiety, annoyance, pressure, etc., cause a shift toward negative potentials, we are justified in assuming that erogenous excitation represents the specifically *productive* process of the living organism. It ought to be possible to verify this in other biological processes, such as cell division, where, concurrent with the biologically productive activity of division, the cell ought also to develop a higher surface charge. *The sexual process, then, is the*

biological-productive energy process per se. Anxiety is the opposite fundamental biological direction, which is congruent with that of dying, without being identical to it.

10. If the assumption that the orgasm is a fundamental life phenomenon is correct, then the corresponding formula of tension → charge → discharge → relaxation must be the *general formula of living functions* and it ought not to apply to inorganic matter. Heart, intestines, lungs, bladder, as well as cell division, function in this biological rhythm.

11. The way in which the sexual (pleasure, biological energy) household is regulated, and the sex-economic relations between individuals, all assume a greater significance than in the past as regards the pathology of organs, and especially as regards the understanding of all diseases, which must be viewed as disorders of vegetative equilibrium; i.e., as biopathies.

Now that we have arrived at the end of these far-reaching and serious conclusions, we must heed the equally serious warning not to allow ourselves to be misled by the interplay of theoretical perspectives into substituting mere mental constructs for reliable clinical empiricism supported by experimental investigation. No less justified is the converse warning that we should put forward correct hypotheses and amend ingrained beliefs in the light of new theories, in order to prevent clinical treatment and experiments from stagnating.

Electrophotographic Data Showing the Reaction of Skin Potential to Specific Emotional and Mechanical Stimuli

In all electrophotos, O = base line or ground potential (g.p.).

V.P. = *Versuchsperson* (experimental subject). It is probable that initials such as BJ, X, Le, etc., identify these persons.

↑ indicates that the indifferent electrode is placed on the subject's right arm; ↓ indicates its site on the left arm.

The bracketed number at the end of each legend refers to the relevant page in the text.

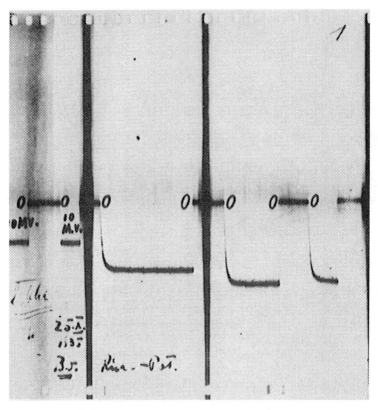

I. Resting potential of average skin [82]

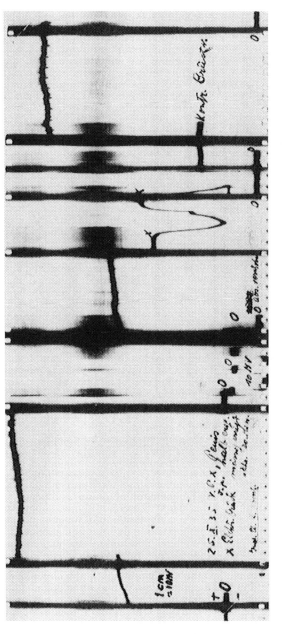

II. Potentials of a semi-erect penis [84]

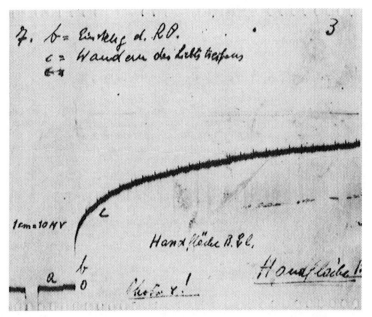

III. "Wandering" of potential on palm of a hand (experienced subjectively as "streaming" of vegetative current) [85]
b = resting potential ceases; c = wandering of light beam

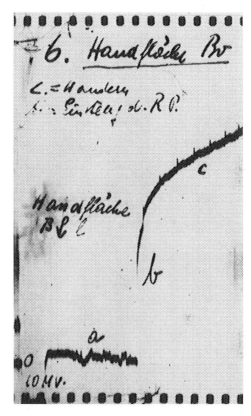

IV. Steeper wandering on the same palm [85]

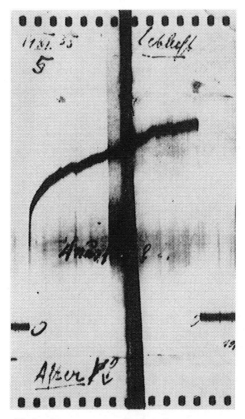

V. Anal mucous membrane of a woman in
a state of excitation [86]

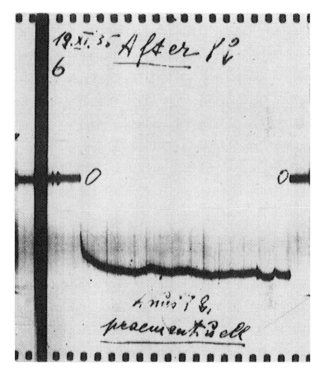

VI. The same in a state of depression (premenstrual) [86]

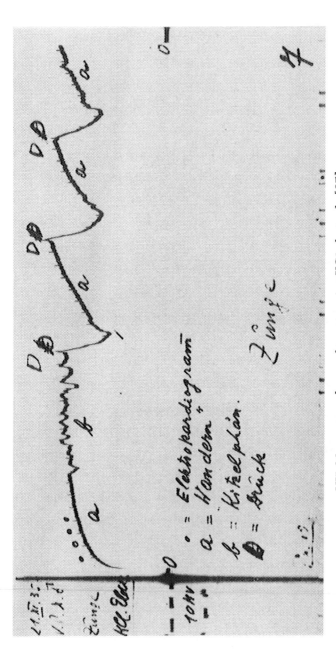

VII. Mucous membrane of tongue using KC1 electrode [87]

○ = electrocardiographic tracing; a = wandering; b = tickling; D = pressure

VIII. Inside of lip, using KCl electrode [89]
K to ✳ = tickling

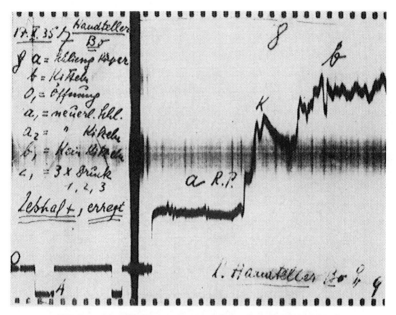

IX. Strong tickling reaction on the palm of a hand [90]
a = circuit closed; R.P. = resting potential;
K = tickling reaction; b = reaction to second tickling stimulus

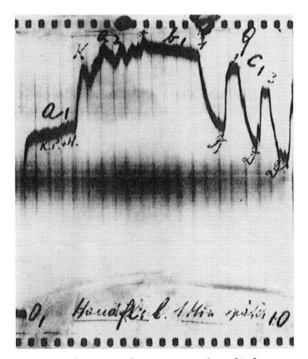

X. The same palm one minute later [90]
O_1 = circuit open; a_1 = circuit closed again;
W = wandering; K = tickling; a_2 = tickling again;
b_1 = no tickling; c_1 = pressure exerted three times;
D = pressure

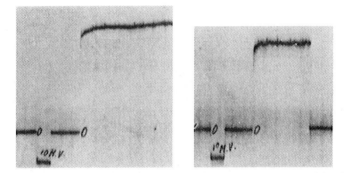

XI. Resting potentials of a right and left palm are symmetrical [91]

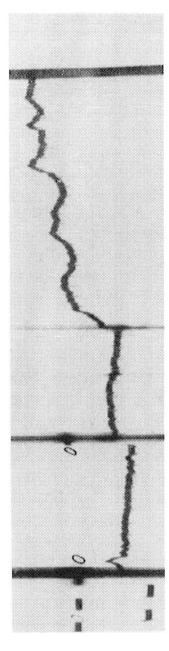

XII. Tickling reaction on the palm of a hand: electrode allowed to rest on skin while adjacent skin area is tickled with cotton wool or a feather [91]

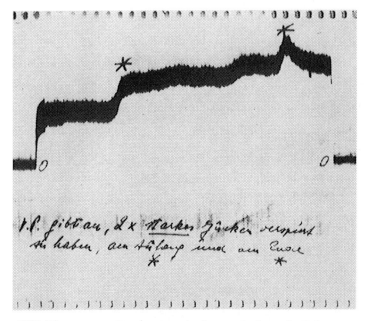

XIII. Pleasure reaction (✳ to ✳) of an excited nipple. Subject experienced strong itching at beginning and end [92]

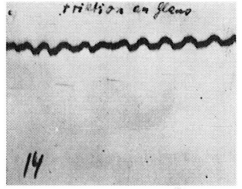

XIV. Friction-induced fluctuations of
potential at glans penis [93]

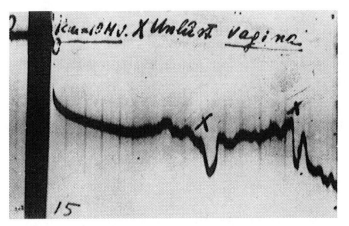

XV. Reaction of vaginal mucous membrane
when subject is annoyed [96]

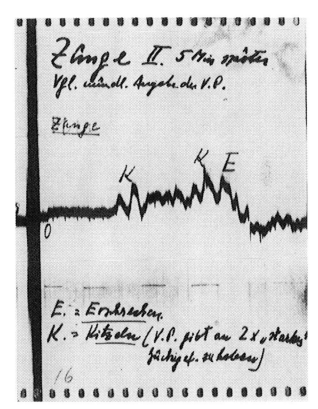

XVI. Reaction of tongue to tickling (K) and fright (E).
Subject reported having twice felt strong itching
with tickling [97]

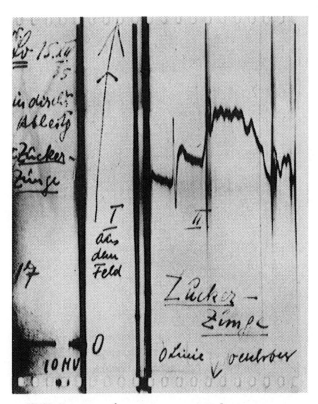

XVII. Reaction of tongue to sugar. Indirect measurement. Indifferent electrode on left arm [100]

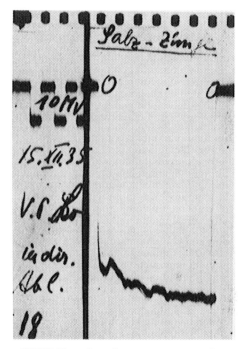

XVIII. Reaction of same tongue to salt.
Indirect measurement. Indifferent electrode
on left arm [101]

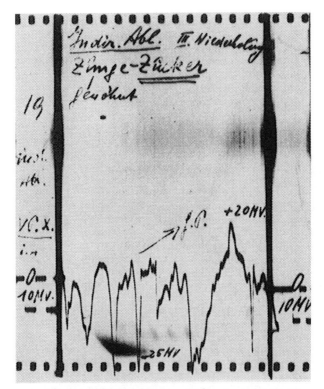

XIX. Sugar reaction of tongue. Indirect measurement.
Indifferent electrode on right arm [103]

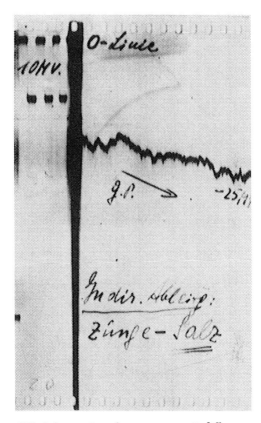

XX. Salt reaction of same tongue. Indifferent
electrode on right arm [103]

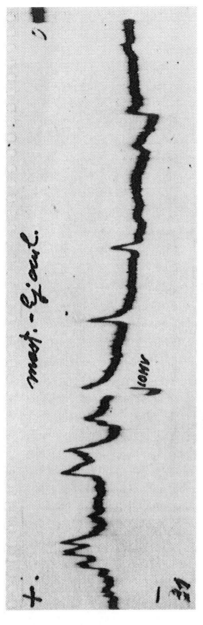

XXI. Excitation during masturbation. Deliberate
interference just before ejaculation [108]

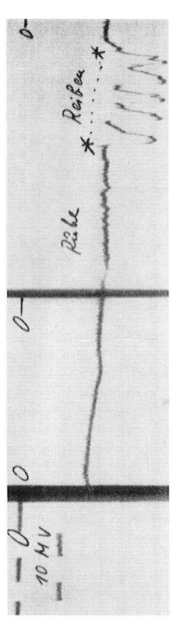

XXII. Contact potential of two fingertips [110]

XXIII. As before, followed by rubbing of fingertip on glass bottom of a container (∗ · · · · ∗) [110]

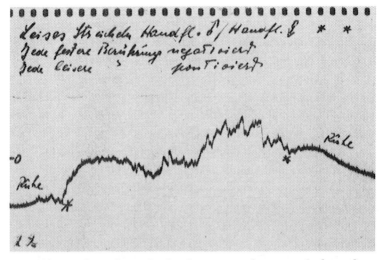

XXIV. Gentle stroking of palms by two people; one with electrode on right arm, the other on left arm (* · · · · *). Every firm touch produces a negative trend; every light touch a positive trend [110]

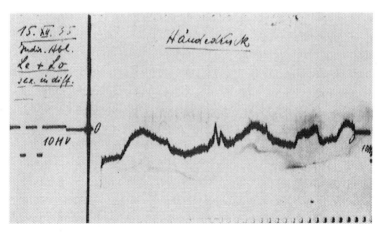

XXV. Stroking of hand alternating with firm handshake. Indirect measurement. Subjects of same sex [111]

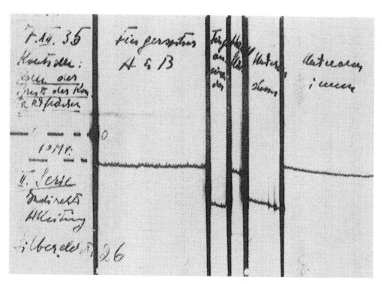

XXVI. Contact potential of various skin surfaces [111]

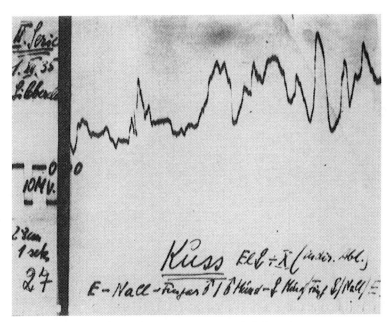

XXVII. Excitation during a kiss [111]

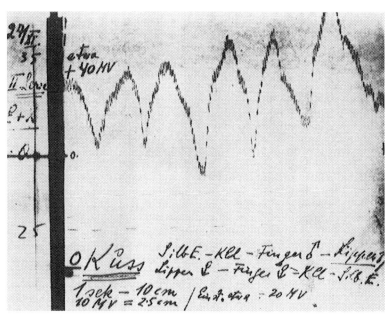

XXVIII. Same, magnified and in slow motion [112]

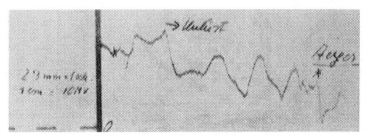

XXIX. Unpleasurable kiss [112]
* = annoyance

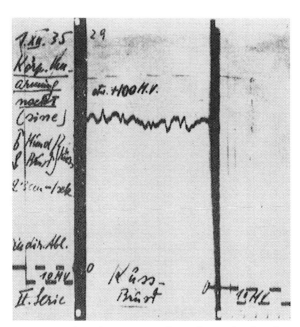

XXX. Naked, embracing couple, with man kissing the
woman's breast. Indirect measurement [112]

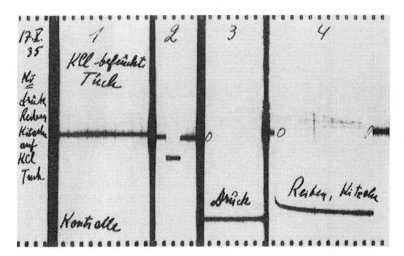

XXXI. Control experiment using KC1-soaked towel [116]
3 = pressure; 4 = rubbing, tickling

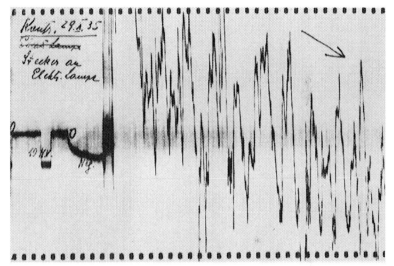

XXXII. Control experiment: rubbing of electrodes on
metal surface of flashlight [117]